Praise for *Embracing Destiny*

"From the heart of a true encourager, Bill Isaacs gives practical insights from the life of Joseph that will strengthen your faith when it seems God has left you alone."

—Tom Madden, Youth Ministries Coordinator
Department of Youth and Christian Education
Church of God, Cleveland, Tennessee

"I commend the author for the practicality of this study and for the challenge it gives us to align ourselves more fully with God's will for our lives—no matter what the circumstances may be."

—T. David Sustar, State Director
Church of God Evangelism and Home Missions
Western North Carolina

"Author Bill Isaacs has done a masterful job of relating the life of Joseph to current issues. Whether it is accepting the victim mentality or lacking the ability to forgive, he walks us through the struggles of Joseph and points out the steps to spiritual victory."

—W.A. Davis
Administrative Bishop
Virginia

"Never before has the life of Joseph been made more practical and applicable. Each page is enlightening and serves as a Bible study in itself. It is not often that you find a book written with such heartfelt inspiration."

—STEPHEN P. DARNELL
Texas State Youth and Christian Education Director

"First-time author, Bill Isaacs, has hit a home run with his book, *Embracing Destiny*. The refreshing insights, balanced Biblical principles and poignant illustrations offered in this book will ring true with every serious seeker of God's will. I highly recommend it to those who wish to find and fulfill their divine destiny."

—CHUCK NOEL
Northern Ohio State Youth
and Christian Education Director

"Bill Isaacs is a great man of God with a God-given ability to make God's Word come alive. His unique way of making life applications illustrate his message of forgiveness and holding to God's promises. This book will inspire readers and give them a greater understanding of God's guidance in their lives."

—SARAH GLOVER, Youth Pastor
Sumiton Church of God
Sumiton, Alabama

EMBRACING DESTINY

EMBRACING DESTINY

LESSONS FROM
— THE LIFE OF JOSEPH —

BILL ISAACS

DEDICATION

I personally dedicate this project to my family:
my wife,
Kathy Lanier Isaacs,
and sons,
Jeremy Christopher and *Jason Patrick,*
whose consistent love and contributions
make my life enjoyable;
and to my father and mother,
Y. Z. and *Judy Isaacs,*
who have shaped my life through their faithful
teaching, love and acceptance;
To each of you whose faith in me as a son, husband,
father and friend have made every day
a new occasion for joy!

TABLE OF CONTENTS

INTRODUCTION

The measure of a man is his life—not his trappings or his titles. The definition of a man is his life—how he lived it, how he managed it, what he was. I believe that and I live by that. One day, my two sons will bury me in the ground and it won't matter where I ministered or what titles I held. What will linger with my two sons will be my life, our relationship, who I was. Long after I'm gone and the wall plaques have been sold in a yard sale, the measure of my life and yours will be how we lived it. That's why Joseph is so interesting to me. The quality of the man is not measured in his lineage or ancestry, but in how he lived. Joseph lived his life in alignment with his Creator and made an incredible mark for his God, the kingdom and his family.

I don't remember when I began to be intrigued by the life of Joseph. However, I can honestly confess no other Biblical character, with the exception of Jesus Christ, has so captured my attention in study and analysis. This book became a reality because I continued to record all these things which came from my constant study of Joseph's life. Actually, this book reflects more than 20 years of intermittent study of Joseph. Much of this material has been preached in the many places where I have been privileged to visit during these years. Much of it has been gleaned from what I felt God was saying to me about Joseph and how his life relates to our culture today. A great deal of what you read is what I have lived and experienced. In retrospect, I can see the hand of God preparing me and teaching me, depositing these treasures into my life as I attempt to walk with Him daily.

There are seven major characters in the Book of Genesis. You can probably name all of them—Adam, Eve, Noah, Abraham,

Isaac, Jacob and Joseph. There is more written about Joseph than any other character in the book. Fourteen chapters of the Bible's first book are devoted to the details and descriptions of his life. However, as I read and study his life, I am not surprised by this. Evidently, there is something God wants us to know about Joseph. His life speaks to us. We can relate to him. As you consider his life, you will see the sovereignty of God at work in the life of a man who loved God supremely. Lest you think Joseph was someone who had it all together, consider these facts:

1. *He did not choose his own parents.* Like every other child born into the world, he did not know who his father and mother were or how his life would be impacted by them. His family was not his greatest asset. Overcoming his family members and their history was his first major hurdle. The genetic connection was a source of stress for Joseph. In order to survive and succeed, Joseph determined not to allow his family to define his character.

2. *His father was a schemer.* Jacob probably learned how to con and scheme from his mother, Rebekah, who was also deceitful. Joseph's uncle, Laban, Rebekah's brother, was a schemer himself, who deceived Joseph's father into marrying Leah, Rebekah's sister, first, although he did not love her. This was a household with a sordid past. Lying, deception and manipulation were the tradition in his family. Joseph was from a large family of 12 sons and one daughter born to Jacob from his two wives and two concubines. His family was not united. There was much distrust and jealousy. This was his beginning—he could easily have followed the family path, but, remarkably, he chose another course. He abandoned his family way of life and sought God's way. It was a difficult decision and not everyone understood Joseph's behavior, but God guided his steps, as He will guide yours, if you will learn the lesson of Joseph and surrender to Him in obedience.

3. *He lost his mother early in life.* Joseph's mother, Rachel, died during the birth of his younger brother, Benjamin. For the rest of his childhood, he was raised by a stepmother and his father. While there is no record of any physical abuse by the adults, he was left to cope in life without his mother. Millions of adults and children, perhaps even you, know how he felt. The comforting, nurturing touch of a mother is an important part of human life. Faced to live without, we are required to adjust. Many do, but it is never easy. The loss is permanent and lingers like a hidden wound, always there and never fully healed.

There is something profoundly unique about Joseph. Although my background is different from his, I have ministered to many people who can relate to his early life. Unfortunately, some were born to parents who did not have their own lives together and the children suffered because of it. Maybe you are one of them, and your life has been marked by experiences and hurts that have scarred you and you cannot seem to recover. If you are one of those persons, I know you can relate to Joseph. He suffered the hatred of his siblings, the betrayal of his family, the rejection of his peers and yet he never lost hope for tomorrow. How can this be?

Some people never recover from one bad experience, but Joseph lived through a period of more than 13 years with one negative circumstance after another, yet he never gave up his believe in God's ultimate plan. Like Joseph, I have met others who have chosen to live above their circumstances, deciding not to allow negative situations to define them.

I know a woman whose past is not pleasant. A man who once promised to love her only, for as long as they both lived, lied. When he decided he loved another woman, he left my friend in a desperate situation, with small children to raise alone. The impact of that compromise still haunts her children, although they are grown and have their own families.

Together, this lady and her family deal with the trauma of grief and pain. They are familiar with loss and sorrow. The cycle of divorce has marked a son and this devoted woman prays and worries for the effect on her grandchildren. She and her second husband have worked, prayed and struggled at times to survive. Financial reversals from investments gone sour and other events have threatened their sanity and peace at times, but they keep going! She once remarked to me, while under the intense pressure of another attack, "You know, sometimes you just have to tell God, 'I can't handle this! I trust You because I know You love me. I don't understand, but I will not be defeated by this.' You move on, knowing that God will take care of you and your family." She is moving on with her life, although the future is hazy from a human perspective. With every day, she finds new hope and faith in God's ultimate handling of life's struggles.

Joseph was also determined to keep going. Because he did, his life is a glorious story of God's divine providence. There are some rocky roads we must travel. It will be gruesome and difficult—a road you are familiar with already.

If there is one thing the life of Joseph teaches us, it is this: *Your circumstances do not have the power to define you.* You can rise above your environment. Regardless of your beginning, you can be the person God destined you to be. That's the message of this book.

Joseph sincerely believed God had placed His divine hand upon his life. The same can be true for you. The final chapters of your life have not yet been written. There is a brighter day ahead. Our sovereign God is working everything together in your life for a higher purpose. You may not see the outcome yet, and at times you may wonder what God has planned, but if you listen closely to the Savior, you will hear His constant reminder, "Don't give up."

I believe there is something in this journey we are about to take that will touch your soul. My life will never be the same as a result of the truths you now hold in your hand. Don't be afraid to look deeply into the life of Joseph. You may find a jewel that will ensure your survival. It has been my prayer from the beginning days of this project that you will not have picked up this book by accident.

FOREWORD

Much of Scripture is about people we can relate to today. The life of Joseph typifies many of the challenges we will experience the 21st century. Therefore, it is beneficial to glean from his example of conflicts and conquests.

Joseph's family was filled with competition and conflict. He was the victim of partiality by his parents and resentment from siblings. He knew the dilemma of recognition and rejection. The triumph of integrity over temptation stands out clearly. The emotional upheaval of broken promises and betrayal tested his moral fiber. According to human judgment, Joseph would have been justified to hold grudges and get even when he could. However, his example of forgiveness is sterling.

Bill Isaacs is highly qualified to write *Embracing Destiny*. His background as the son of a pastor exposed him to the real world. Growing up in church work in North Carolina involved him in the trials and triumphs of everyday life. Local church parsonages are the gathering ground for a potpourri of problems and victories as the minister struggles to assist the parishioners in understanding how to cope with life.

Bill was a normal preacher's kid who filtered the pros and cons of life and cast his lot with Christ. He struggled, but survived. His wife, Kathy, and two sons, Jeremy and Jason, have contributed to the preparation for this book in their journey as a family. The family has been challenged, but they learned to conquer through Christ and the power of the Spirit.

This writing evolved out of the daily school of life in the author's experience. He served as pastor of a local church, thereby gaining insight into the complexity of defining individuality in life. He understands that every individual is on a particular journey. He has served very successfully for many years as the leader of youth and Christian education ministry in several states. His roles have demanded a cutting-edge awareness of the dilemma children, youth and adults face in determining their destiny. However, understanding what to do leads to the problem of the journey to reach the goal.

Embracing destiny is a process. Bill's tremendous ability in assisting young people to sort through all the stuff they face helps chart a successful course to their own destiny. Being a parent himself has augmented his study relative to destiny and how it is embraced. As a student of Scripture, he is convinced that God has a will for every life.

The author has chosen a prototypical example in Joseph, the son of Jacob in the Old Testament, around which to form his thesis. Joseph had a multiplicity of experiences in his journey for destiny that correlate to persons in all generations. Isaacs' unique ability allowed him to bring Joseph in relationship to our present time. The reader will discover a close kinship with the struggling figure of ancient past. Isaacs understands that times have changed, but God, human nature and demonic design have not.

Readers will identify with the highs and lows of Joseph's road. They will be able to understand that, like Joseph,

- They too will make mistakes trying to embrace their destiny.

- They will understand that their mistakes are not far removed from young Joseph's pride over a pretty coat and dreams of being a great leader.

- They will relate to the pit experience of rejection and alienation because of jealousy.

It will be easy to get a sense of having truth rejected, even though temptation was overcome.

Suffering for something which you are not guilty of is an opportunity to give up and never try again. But read on and learn that faithfulness pays off. People may forget and desert you, but God is faithful.

Readers will sense the depths of disappointment and scale the heights of victory as they are taken on the journey of Joseph. It is set forth clearly in this book that God has a desired destiny for every life. Like Joseph, each individual must embrace the destiny through the daily journey. It may lead through the pit, but there is a royal place awaiting each person who is faithful on the journey.

Embracing Destiny is written in a style that gives insight from the life of Joseph and relates these insights to children, siblings, parents and every member of the family. It focuses on teaching and discussion for youth and other groups.

These are days when multitudes of people feel lost and can't seem to find their direction. This is evidenced by the tremendous restlessness that exists. Many wonder if anyone cares. God cared for Joseph and He cares for you. My prayer is that as you read this book, you will have a new sense of personal direction through the Holy Spirit.

May I personally commend my friend for the work that he has brought to us, which is evidently the product of the anointing of the Holy Spirit. He is to be appreciated for taking the time and making the effort to share.

Thanks, Bill!

—Walter P. Atkinson

*And his brothers saw that their father
loved him more than all his brothers;
and so they hated him
and could not speak to him
on friendly terms.*
Genesis 37:4

CHAPTER ONE

WHEN YOUR FAMILY IS THE ENEMY

To really know a person, you have to know a little about their family and upbringing. If you want to know what a person is genuinely like, go home and meet the family. Likewise, if we want to get acquainted with Joseph, we need to take a close look at his family. Let me warn you, it may not be a pleasant experience. Unfortunately, it looks very much like many families today. If you look closely, you will see the ugliness of selfishness, petty jealousy, envy and hatred. This was not "home sweet home." Joseph's family was the textbook definition of dysfunctional.

His father, Jacob, was the twin brother of Esau, and son of Isaac and Rebekah. From his mother's influence, Jacob learned to maneuver and manipulate people. It was his mother who schemed with him to steal his older brother's blessing from their father. He did so, and, as a result of Esau's commitment of revenge toward him, Jacob fled. At his mother's urging, Jacob traveled to live with her brother, Laban.

Rebekah also came from a family of deceivers. Laban made a deal with Jacob for the hand of his younger daughter, Rachel. However, after working seven years to win his bride, Jacob found himself waking up beside Rachel's older sister, Leah, whom he did not love. The con man had been conned.

The Bible never indicates that Jacob ever loved Leah. She was not his choice for a wife. However, because of Laban's trickery, Jacob, Leah and their children were never truly fulfilled in their family life. Jacob eventually worked seven more years to marry Rachel, his true love, but Laban's earlier deceit profoundly affected Jacob's entire family.

Jacob fathered a total of 13 children. Twelve sons and one daughter were born to him from Leah, Rachel, and his two concubines, Bilhah and Zilpah. While they all had the same father, they were certainly not a family unit. The dysfunction of this family is the result of several stress points that require a closer look.

RACHEL AND LEAH'S INTENSE RIVALRY

Rachel was Jacob's choice for a wife, but, because of his uncle's deception, Leah was Jacob's first wife. Both women were highly competitive and the birth of children was seen by them as the way to gain favor in the eyes of Jacob.

So Jacob went in to Rachel also, and indeed he loved Rachel more than Leah. . . . [Leah] conceived again and bore a son and said, "Now this time my husband will become attached to me, because I have borne him three sons.". . . Now when Rachel saw that she bore Jacob no children, she became jealous of her sister; and she said to Jacob, "Give me children, or else I die." (Genesis 29:30, 34; 30:1).

There is something profoundly wrong with this household. Jacob's superior feelings for Rachel are a precursor of his subsequent partiality concerning his children. The favoritism he practiced with his wives was carried on to his sons. This preferential treatment caused intense strife and feelings of hatred between the brothers.

RACHEL'S PREMATURE DEATH

Rachel's death, recorded in Genesis 35:18, 19, was untimely and premature. It came at the birth of her second son, Benjamin, Joseph's only full brother. Jacob had just moved the family caravan from Bethel where he communed with God and heard God recommit to the covenant relationship established with Jacob's grandfather, Abraham. Rachel died while Joseph was still a young boy. Although we are not told how he dealt with the loss of his mother, we can be certain that her death changed the dynamics of the household.

Thousands of years later, we are still learning the effects on children who must face life without either or both of their natural parents. No matter where you go or what becomes of your life, there is no one in your life quite like your mother. Big football players in the NFL stand on the sidelines and wave in to the camera, "Hi, Mom!" Regardless of anyone's lot in life, Mother always holds a special place in the heart of a child. When you lose your mother, regardless of your age, the loss is profound. I've seen grown men cry and struggle with the loss of an aged mother who had, long ago, given up the primary responsibility for their care. The emotional bond is strong.

Joseph's mother was gone. We don't know much about the relationship between Leah and Rachel's children. At best, stepmother/child relationships require work. Leah had children of her own, and she was painfully aware of the fact that Jacob had never intended to marry her. Rachel had been his choice. We can't know if Leah mistreated Joseph and his brother, and any speculation on the quality of their relationship would be biased, based on stereotypes and personal experience regarding stepfamilies. In any case, Joseph's life was affected by the fragmented condition of his family.

JACOB'S FAVORITE (GENESIS 37:3)
Joseph held a special place in his father's heart because he was the firstborn son of Rachel, his true love. As a result of his affection, Jacob made him a coat of many colors. The coat was evidence of a special and exclusive relationship. Because the brothers knew their father loved Joseph more than he loved them, they were infuriated.

Preferential treatment of one child over another always creates turmoil. Family relationships were strained because Jacob did not love his children equally, though they all

22

wanted and deserved his love. Since the Bible never says that Jacob loved Leah, the children of Leah probably resented their father's attachments to Joseph, Benjamin and Rachel. Anyone who has been in this situation can understand the hot sting of resentment that must have constantly tortured Joseph's brothers. As a caring parent, you should desire to love all your children equally and never allow any of your children to feel they are loved less than another sibling. Any other course of action paves the way for bitterness and disillusionment.

Divorce has broken the hearts of too many children who were forced to live in hostile environments. Even where there is an honest and loving attempt to blend families, the process is difficult. Stepchildren and step-parents often struggle to maintain a proper balance in their relationships. Some children grow up resenting a father who abandoned his family or a mother who chose to leave her children in the care of another person. Such circumstances have long-term effects on a child's psyche.

Years ago, I had a friend whose parents no longer lived together. A messy divorce had separated their family. When I first met John, he and his older brother lived with their mom and her new husband, but the relationship was not good. The previous family had been churchgoing and the boys' extended family members were all Christians. The new family did not attend church. Their lifestyle included drinking, partying and other activities foreign to these children. Fighting was common and the boys often found themselves in the middle. In the end, both boys moved away from their parents. The older brother eventually stayed with grandparents, but John drifted.

Sometimes, he would sleep on my couch. Both boys battled the unending question "Why?"

The talks I had with John and his brother centered around the *why* questions. John, especially, longed for his dad to express his love and affection. The father, who had suffered his own emotional losses, struggled to put the pieces together for his sons. He truly loved his sons, but his new wife had plans for her own family.

I believe these boys bore unmistakable marks of rejection that haunted them throughout life. With sadness and regret, they had to pick up some heavy baggage from the hurts inflicted by their parents. Many can relate to this burning sensation in the heart that never completely healed. This was no justification for their future actions, but we can see they were not entirely at fault. Jacob could have done better by his children.

Because of his special relationship with his father, Joseph evidently did not have to work like his other brothers, as we read in Genesis 37:13, 14. While they tended the flocks in the hot desert sun, Joseph was at home with his father. At evening, when his brothers returned home, Joseph was babbling about his dreams, which told of his exaltation over his brothers. No wonder they hated him.

Adam Clarke gives the following insight into Genesis 37:4:

> Does not this imply, in our use of the term, that they were continually quarreling with him? . . . They could not speak peace to him, i.e., they would not accost him in a friendly manner. They would not even wish him

well. The eastern method of salutation is, Peace be to thee! among the Hebrews, and salam, peace, or peace to thee my friend, among the Arabs. Now as peace among those nations comprehends all kinds of blessings spiritual and temporal, so they are careful not to say it to those whom they do not cordially wish well. It is not an unusual thing for an Arab or a Turk to hesitate to return the salam, if given by a Christian, or by one of whom he has not a favorable opinion: and this, in their own country, may be ever considered as a mark of hostility; not only as a proof that they do not wish you well, but that if they have an opportunity they will do you an injury. This was precisely the case with respect to Joseph's brethren: they would not give him the salam, and therefore felt themselves at liberty to take the first opportunity to injure him.

There is obvious resentment from the other brothers toward Joseph. In their eyes, he was getting away with murder, and they were paying for his comfort.

Remember how Martha resented Mary, her sister, who was not slaving over the meal preparations when Jesus came to visit? We have all been there. While working hard, you notice someone sitting idly by, thumbing through a magazine. It's only natural to feel resentment.

A PASSIVE FATHER (GENESIS 35)

Because of Jacob's passivity toward his family, things went untended. This added to the frustration of his sons. Two separate instances indicate this passivity. In one instance, Dinah, the daughter of Leah, was raped by Shechem, the son of Hamor the Hivite (Genesis 34). Apparently, her father did nothing about it! Subsequently, the sons of Leah devised a plan and deceived the Hivites who fell into the trap. The sons of Jacob slaughtered the men in the city in retaliation for the rape of their sister.

When Jacob heard about it, he was angry, but not about the rape. His anger centered on how actions of his sons would affect his business relationships with the people of the land.

In another instance, Reuben had sexual relations with Jacob's concubine, Bilhah (35:22). The Bible implies that Jacob did nothing about it. He knew exactly what Reuben had done, because he mentioned it in detail in Genesis 49:4, when he gave his blessing to Reuben. This passivity fostered rebellion and distrust.

The Bible indicates that the brothers could not speak peaceably to Joseph. There was a boiling cauldron about to erupt. Their frustration was obvious and Jacob was unresponsive.

Perhaps Jacob did not know what to do. It does not matter. Children are gifts from the Lord, and responsible parents must treat them as such. Children cannot help the circumstances under which they are brought into the world, but they deserve to be loved intensely, supported unconditionally and parented responsibly. If Jacob had realized this, it could have saved his children many problems throughout their lives.

Sometimes our family is not the refuge God intended it to be. Perhaps you struggle to keep feelings of resentment, or even hatred, at bay. You are not alone. Sometimes our only peace is when we are away from our family. We harbor bitterness over broken family relationships, often seeking ways to avoid talking to one another. Strained relationships in our family strike at the very core of the soul.

Hatred is a strong emotion. It is mentioned as one of the "works of the flesh" in Galatians 5:19, 20 (KJV). The Bible indicates that Joseph's brothers hated him. The end result was an abhorrent act of betrayal.

Some time ago, I watched a trial on TV involving a woman accused of two vicious murders. Her husband had left her and remarried. The unfaithfulness of his actions, the court-ordered surrender of her custodial rights to their children and her inability to move on with her life pushed this woman to a breaking point. According to her testimony, this educated socialite broke into the house of her former husband and ruthlessly shot him and his wife at close range. She looked refined and elegant on the stand, but the hatred in her heart motivated her to commit an unthinkable crime.

Even the best of families have problems, possibly severe problems. Some years ago, there was an attempt to identify the ideal American family. After an exhaustive search, a family from the suburbs of Houston, Texas, was chosen. The mother was an investment accountant, the father a real estate broker. They had three children, each enrolled in private schools. They had a home in the city and one on the lake. They had enough cars, money and social connections to make life pleasurable and meaningful. They appeared to be the ideal family—until the end came.

One day, as the husband arrived home, he noticed an eerie silence in the house instead of the normal hustle and bustle. Moving upstairs, he discovered two of the children dead from multiple stab wounds and the third was barely conscious. The child whispered, "Daddy, Mommy's gone crazy."

As he held the dying child, he heard a blood-curdling scream from the pool. Racing to the window, he saw his wife fall into the pool, the knife with which she had stabbed herself still in her chest. Evidently, the pressures of life had overwhelmed her.

There is no security for any family outside of the grace and peace of God. The later stories of Jacob's family include acts of murder, incest and other atrocities—all the result of abandoning godly principles of living. One son committed incest with his own daughter-in-law. Others became belligerent men who preyed on innocent people.

It is remarkable to realize that from this family would come a young man whose heart yearned only for God—a young man whose passion and pursuit of God became his salvation. Joseph never allowed his circumstances or adversaries to dim his focus. He kept his eyes squarely on the prize of God's ultimate and glorious plan for his life.

In the summer of 1990, I preached at a youth camp in Atlanta, Georgia. One night, while preaching about David and Goliath, I challenged the teens to realize that, like David, God had great plans for their lives. Many teens moved toward the altar, and I believe some eternal decisions were made. One boy in particular remarked to me about how much he wanted to be what I had preached about. But there was a problem, he said. His father had left his mother for another woman and was living with her near their home. "So I can't be what you preached about, can I?" he asked.

Trying not to show any shock at his revelation about his father, I said, "It really doesn't matter if your dad left your mom. You can be what I was talking about."

He seemed more confused. "But you need to know that my brother is in prison for selling dope to an undercover officer. He will be there for quite a while."

"It doesn't matter," I said. "These things have nothing to do with what God has planned for you. He invites you to be a mighty giant-killer for God." After staring at me for a moment, he burst into tears. I believe the Holy Spirit opened his eyes to see that no person or circumstance can keep us from being what God wants us to be. But we must stay focused on the Lord and His plans.

> Who shall separate us from the love of Christ? Shall tribulation, or distress, or persecution, or famine, or nakedness, or peril, or sword? Just as it is written: "For Thy sake we are being put to death all day long; we are considered as sheep to be slaughtered." But in all these things we overwhelmingly conquer through Him who loved us. For I am convinced that neither death, nor life, nor angels, nor principalities, nor things present, nor things to come, nor powers, nor height, nor depth, nor any other created thing, shall be able to separate us from the love of God, which is in Christ Jesus our Lord (Romans 8:35-39).

It is interesting to see that Joseph's family did not understand the significance of his dreams. As you read the dialogue, you sense that they were talking on two different levels. Joseph saw the future and believed his dreams confirmed it. His brothers saw their younger sibling, whom they hated, boasting of some perceived superiority over them. Their father questioned the validity of Joseph's dream and tried to temper the possibilities they inferred. This did not stop Joseph—he believed what God had shown him.

It is never easy to realize your dreams when your family does not support you. Joseph's brothers could not see the future because of the bitterness of their past. Maybe you have struggled to gain your family's support of your dreams. If so, you can take heart in the reality that if you truly love the Lord, your dreams are important to Him.

In His given time, God can work everything out. Despite the bad mistakes of your past, you have now turned the corner in your life, and God is opening a new chapter. If God is at work, He will work on family members. And time is your greatest ally. While it is true the present is marred by the past, God can do remarkable things with our memories—as Joseph's life proves. These principles will help you find peace in relationships with your family as you pursue God.

WHAT YOU ALLOW TO DEFINE YOU

Joseph's family had problems, like any other family. Although we cannot choose our parents—that's a privilege only God has—your parents do not have to define your life.

Jimmy, an anointed youth pastor, came to my office one afternoon without an appointment, but it was obvious he had something tugging at his heart. He needed to talk and he had decided to share with me the background of his family. A neglectful father and siblings who had lived in open sin had marked their family with undeniable turmoil and pain. Drugs and riotous living was the way of life for everyone in his house, except Jimmy. "I decided not to follow that path," he said. "My family has been marked by a long line of sin, but I am determined that is not the way for me and my family!"

As tears rolled down his face and he struggled to maintain his composure, I realized that, like Joseph, Jimmy had decided not to be defined by what his family had done. Instead, he placed his life in the hands of a God who can turn any situation around. He was not "Jimmy, the son of a drunk." Rather, he was Jimmy, a faithful husband and father, determined to pursue God. Joseph did the same thing. He loved his family and he did not forsake them. He simply did not allow their actions and words to distract him. His direction came from God.

GOD'S ABILITY TO RESTORE AND HEAL

If we can believe and embrace this principle, we have hope. For some, this moment brings terrible memories of yesterday—feelings of hurt, resentment, anger and even rage. These emotions drive a wedge between family members. We need restoration. God specialized in working out unworkable situations to glorious ends. When we feel there is no resolution to a situation, God steps in and brings healing. Kindness and love replace the brokenness. Don't try to work it out yourself. Just quietly bow your head and commit the past, present and future of your family situation to Him. Then stand back and wait. You might be truly amazed at the end result of His handiwork.

REACHING YOUR DESTINY

Ultimately, I am responsible for only one person—me. I get stressed when I start trying to be responsible for more than I should. God allows His creation to determine which path to take in life. Some choose roads of destruction that bring sadness to their lives and the lives of those who love them. Realizing their own responsibility for their dilemma does not remove the consequential pain. Our culture tends to assign blame for every problem to some global evil. But many times the simple truth is that people choose their own paths—some overlook the consequences and are forced to suffer.

GOD CARES

When life is at its worst, God is at His best! God has never lost sight of who you are or where you are going. In times of despair and loneliness, when you cry yourself to sleep, He is your constant companion. The apostle Peter's words are important during these times: "[Cast] all your care upon Him, for He cares for you" (1 Peter 5:7, NKJV).

If your family situation is like Joseph's, there is still hope for you. Your unfortunate circumstances can change. The good news is that God has a plan for your life. He invites you to step out of the dark cloud of your family troubles and stand tall in the revealed promises of God. Today is a new day. As you read these words from Jeremiah 29:11, remember the promise is for you! "'For I know the plans that I have for you,' declares the Lord, 'plans for welfare and not for calamity to give you a future and a hope." So keep looking up—God is writing a beautiful masterpiece and you are the main character. Trust Him—He has a plan for you.

*A*nd Judah said to his brothers, "What profit is it for us to kill our brother and cover up his blood? Come and let us sell him to the Ishmaelites and not lay our hands on him; for he is our brother, our own flesh." And his brothers listened to him. . . . So they pulled him up and lifted Joseph out of the pit, and sold him to the Ishmaelites for twenty shekels of silver. Thus they brought Joseph into Egypt.

Genesis 37:26-28

CHAPTER TWO

WHEN YOU ARE BETRAYED

Sometimes you only get one chance and a wrong choice can forever alter the course of your life. Some people never get another chance to right a wrong. One man's life was forever marked by one such bad decision. Negative thoughts are always associated with this man, whose fame resulted from his choice to betray the Revolutionary cause in our nation's fight for independence. This act of treason marked Benedict Arnold as a "traitor" to his countrymen and determined his legacy in history. All the good things he did in his life are lost in the memory of this one despicable act.

There is no emotion quite like the feeling of betrayal. As I have read the story of Joseph through the years, nothing strikes me with more emotion than the betrayal of Joseph's own brothers when they sold him to the

Ishmaelites. Jealousy over their father's relationship with Joseph and his insensitivity to their needs and feelings drove Joseph's brothers to this drastic act. It was a conspiracy that would stay with this family for many years.

Betrayal is not easily forgotten. The hurt is obvious and the questions are many. We can only wonder what went through Joseph's mind as he traveled to Egypt in the caravan that evening. Did he cry? Was he broken? What could possibly have motivated his brothers to sell him?

I have two brothers. One died as an infant, but he has always been part of my life and memories. My younger brother, Tim, was born 10 years after me, so we have had different interests and our moments of difficulty. Like all siblings, at times I wanted to "knock his block off." I wanted him to leave me alone . . . stay out of my room . . . stay out of my life! But I never wanted to sell him! I loved him. How would you live with yourself? How do you give up something that is part of who you are? Through the fusses, fights, feuds, I promise you that selling Tim never crossed my mind.

In the previous chapter, we learned that the hatred from Joseph's brothers prevented them from speaking peaceably with him. We can relate to that. But selling their brother? What a coldhearted decision! Actually, it was an alternative choice. Their first plan was to kill him. Read the words of Genesis 37:18-20, describing their plot.

> When they saw him from a distance and before he came close to them, they plotted against him to put him to death. And they said to one another, "Here comes this

dreamer! Now then, come and let us kill him and throw him into one of the pits; and we will say, 'A wild beast devoured him.' Then let us see what will become of his dreams!"

Fortunately for Joseph, an older brother, Reuben, prevailed with a scheme of his own: "Reuben further said to them, 'Shed no blood. Throw him into this pit that is in the wilderness, but do not lay hands on him'—that he might rescue him out of their hands, to restore him to his father" (v. 22).

So it came about, when Joseph reached his brothers, that they stripped Joseph of his tunic, the varicolored tunic that was on him; and they took him and threw him into the pit. Now the pit was empty, without any water in it (vv. 23, 24).

We are not told how long Joseph was in the pit with no water or food. He knew how his brothers felt about him. He may have realized that he was partly to blame for their antagonism toward him. Joseph's security in his father's relationship had been flaunted in his brothers' faces. He never tried to bridge the gap. However, as he sat in the pit, he was stunned and bewildered. He had driven his brothers wild with his visions, dreams and speculations, but he never thought they would try to kill him. What about the dreams? What about God's plan? How did this happen?

We have all been touched by some form of betrayal. For some, it seems trivial, but for others, emotions are already stirring, causing ugly feelings to rise to the surface. You thought you had overcome them, they pop up at the most unexpected times. You *know* what Joseph felt in that pit. You are familiar with the questions and the feelings of discomfort as your mind begins to relive the pain and disappointment. Maybe you can remember when . . .

- He said he would love you and you alone. But the note on the table says he's not coming back. He asks for a divorce, and his attorney's card is stapled to the note.

- She said she would always be your best friend, but now she's taken your place with him.

- It was your idea. He listened to you share it over dinner, then he took it to the boss and got the assignment.

- You shared something very personal and believed everyone understood it was confidential. Now you're embarrassed beyond belief, and deeply hurt that someone you trusted betrayed you.

Nearly everyone has felt the bitter sting of disappointment and betrayal and, just like Joseph, we all have to deal with the hurt. There will be no peace until we settle this issue.

A wise friend once told me, "When someone trusts you, it is a heavier weight than when they don't!" Broken trust may never be fully restored. Watch marriage partners struggle to regain their relationship after dealing with unfaithfulness. It's indescribably difficult. Observe the businessman, whose partners sold him out for a large profit, struggle to even speak peaceably with them again. Anger is inevitable when faced with betrayal. Emotions run deep. People will forgive, but they are more careful the next time when they have to trust you. When a spouse is unfaithful to you, forgiveness is the correct response, but trust is always harder than forgiveness.

I know people who say you have not truly forgiven until you trust again. That may be true, but there is no question that trust requires an extra portion of grace. God enabled Joseph to completely forgive his brothers. God can do remarkable things with a heart willing to forgive.

Several years ago, I was the victim of vicious criticism by two men I trusted and believed in. Although I am not usually sensitive to such things, there was something in this act that hurt to the core. When I overheard these men talking about me, enumerating my inabilities and shortcomings, I was wounded. To my knowledge, they never knew I was around the corner. To this day, I doubt they even recall their words. Unfortunately, I do. When it happened, I quietly left the building and started home. Only God and I knew what was in my heart. Hot tears rolled down my cheeks and my heart screamed, "Why me?"

The only time in my life I believe I saw a vision was in the car driving home that afternoon. In the vision, there was a beautiful bowl of fruit on a kitchen counter. I saw a body move past the bowl and accidently knock it off the counter. The bowl and fruit came crashing to the floor. While I saw no faces, I heard a voice say, "Pick it up and put it back into the bowl. Nothing is hurt."

The voice was wrong. The fruit had been bruised from the fall. If you place a bruised apple in a bowl with healthy fruit, no one would notice—for a while. But over time, the apple would decay. If you left it in the bowl long enough, the other fruit would rot as well.

As I drove, the Holy Spirit began to speak to my heart, "That's what will happen to you if you allow this bruise to go unattended."

"But it's not my fault," I protested. "I didn't do anything to them."

"Even so, the bruise is yours to deal with. It is your spirit that will be affected." Then I remembered the words of Jesus, "The Spirit of the Lord is upon me, because he hath anointed me . . . to set at liberty them that are bruised" (Luke 4:18, KJV). I realized the Lord would have to help me deal with my bruise.

"That's what I want!" I cried with all my heart. Supernaturally, the Lord touched me in that car. By the time I got home, I was a different person. I still remember the experience, but I am not negatively affected by it anymore, because the Lord set me free from the bruise I had suffered.

Sadly that is what happened to some of you. The bitterness of a betrayal in the past destroyed your fruitfulness. Over time, you have unintentionally allowed the incident to dominate your life until you cannot be free from it. Bitterness and rottenness claimed your soul. You find yourself treating everyone differently because of the hurt. They did not hurt you, but they bear the brunt of your frustration. The bitterness has eaten away at your spirit and tainted your outlook.

It happens every day—people who are bruised from life's hurts and betrayals want to get better, but they fail to allow Jesus to heal the wounds. Day after day, the hurt becomes a part of who they are. Years later, they seek vindication, revenge, or anything that will regain their reputation, money or relationship. The rottenness of the bruise spreads, leaving a bitter person in its wake.

There is hope. Remember, the Savior can release you! I can personally attest to the power of that release and what happens when we allow the Holy Spirit to cleanse and free us. Jesus said it like this: "If therefore the Son shall make you free, you shall be free indeed" (John 8:36).

The answer lies in your ability to focus on the Savior and not on the hurt. I know it is hard, and I am not trying to deny your pain, your hurt or their obligation to make things right. But you must be released from your despair so you can be what God wants you to be. The Savior is standing at your heart's door, knocking and inviting you to step out of your closet of hurt and walk in the freedom of release. Once you step out, you will find freedom.

I don't remember where I first saw the slogan that says, "When bad things happen, I have two choices—let it make me *better* or *bitter*." Several years ago, I met a young couple who were blessed with a wonderful little daughter, Haile. As she approached her first birthday, it became apparent that there was something physically wrong with Haile. After multiple tests and consultations, her family was told that Haile had a rare childhood disease—death was certain. The last days of her life were difficult, and her parents and extended family members struggled to come to grips with the tragedy.

How do you resolve those tough issues? Through the days and weeks since Haile's death, I have watched this couple continue their journey out of the dark valley of death. The hurt is not over and some feelings will remain forever, but God is giving them strength as they lean on Him and each other.

At some point, we must come to this realization—if God is in control of our lives, He will take care of us. One man writes, "Eventually, you will have to make peace with the sovereignty of God. Either God is in control or He is not. You must decide which you believe is true."[1]

It does not change the facts, but it helps the healing. The prophet Isaiah wrote:

> Shout for joy, O heavens! And rejoice, O earth! Break forth into joyful shouting, O mountains! For the Lord has comforted His people, and will have compassion on His afflicted. But Zion said, "The Lord has forsaken me, and the Lord has forgotten me. Can a woman forget her nursing child, and have no compassion on the son of her womb? Even these may forget, but I will not forget you. Behold I have inscribed you on the palms of My hands; your walls are continually before Me" (Isaiah 49:13-16).

Your hurts are not lost on the Lord. He sees and understands what you feel. He stands ready to help you resolve those feelings of bewilderment and disappointment by offering you a fresh glimpse of Him—the Savior.

When seen in the light of His love and compassion for you, all bitterness will be released. This was the message of the apostle Peter to the weary saints of Asia Minor:

> In this you greatly rejoice, even though now for a little while, if necessary, you have been distressed by various trials, that the proof of your faith, being more precious than gold which is perishable, even though tested by fire, may be found to result in praise and glory and honor at the revelation of Jesus Christ; and though you have not see Him, you love Him, and though you do not see Him now, but believe in Him, you greatly rejoice with joy inexpressible and full of glory, obtaining as the outcome of your faith the salvation of your souls (1 Peter 1:6-9).

Joseph's life is not much different from yours and mine. Life is about dealing with issues and handling them with grace and faith. No one gets a free ride. The tough part is that not everyone plays by the rules. Hurt is inevitable. So what are we supposed to do?

1. *Tell God about it.* In his book, *Visioneering* , Pastor Andy Stanley writes about criticism. The principle applies to us as well.

> That emotion must go somewhere. To reflect it back on our critics is to play their game. To bottle it up inside can result in depression or ulcers. Another option is to dump it out on someone completely unrelated to the situation: spouse, friends, employees, your children. That only complicates things. The only healthy and profitable thing to do is to pour out your heart to your heavenly Father. . . . After all, he knows what is in your heart anyway. And hey, he's been around. He can handle a little venting. He is honored when we take our deepest frustrations and hurts to him. To do so is an expression of trust.[2]

2. *Talk with someone you trust.* When your load is heavy, don't bear it alone—confide in someone. Once I read that a friend is someone to whom you can tell anything without them feeling any differently toward you. Everyone needs someone like that—someone who will not judge your disposition as evil.

Joseph must have spent his days contemplating his circumstances and the events that led up to them. Yet, he never allowed this contemplation to make him a bitter person. In the pit there was no one to listen to Joseph's troubles. Later that evening, the road to Egypt was lonely as well. He meant nothing to the men except what he would bring in the slave market. He must have thought he would never return home.

GIFT OF HEALING
There is a hand extended to you right now. You have not gone too far. You have not missed your opportunity. God opened this door, right now, as you read this book, to say, "Come, let's deal with this!" Only God can truly heal you. Others can help, offering their faith and confidence, but only God can heal. He is faithful in every storm to bring peace and calm your soul. That's His gift!

MEMORY OF THE PAST
Today's trials are only temporary. The words of a song by Bill Gaither say: "It won't rain always." Keep that in mind. Maintain your integrity and faith in God. Don't let what happened yesterday change the promise of today. There is freshness in each moment God provides. Each day holds great potential, and if you believe in Him, He

has a way of making today a new experience of hope and joy.

Somehow, Joseph knew better than to allow one day to ruin his life. He had a dream from the Lord. He had a destiny to fulfill and he intended to embrace it—whatever the cost! Remember, he didn't know how the story would end!

God was working His plan for Joseph, his father Jacob, and even his 10 deceitful brothers. God always has a plan. He does for you. Be patient and wait. He will do his work in you! "For I am confident of this very thing, that He who began a good work in you will perfect it until the day of Christ Jesus" (Philippians 1:6).

Now Joseph had been taken down to Egypt; and Potiphar, an Egyptian officer of Pharaoh, the captain of the bodyguard, bought him from the Ishmaelites, who had taken him down there. And the Lord was with Joseph, so he became a successful man. And he was in the house of his master, the Egyptian. Now his master saw that the Lord was with him and how the Lord caused all that he did to prosper in his hand. So Joseph found favor in his sight, and became his personal servant; and he made him overseer over his house, and all that he owned he put in his charge. And it came about that from the time he made him overseer in his house, and over all that he owned, the Lord blessed the Egyptian's house on account of Joseph; thus the Lord's blessing was upon all that he owned, in the house and in the field. So he left everything he owned in Joseph's charge; and with him there he did not concern himself with anything except the food which he ate. Now Joseph was handsome in form and appearance.

Genesis 39:1-6

CHAPTER THREE

WHEN ALL YOU CAN DO IS BE FAITHFUL

How we handle adversity says a great deal about our maturity as believers. So how do we handle adversity? It is important to avoid the pattern of accepting something just because it feels good. If it feels bad, is it inherently bad? This is not how faith works. We cannot allow circumstances, whether positive or negative, to determine our worth. God's ways are higher. As His children, we must trust His greater knowledge and find peace in the reality of His higher purpose.

When we consider Joseph at this point in his life, we can't help but feel compassion for someone whose whole life had been changed by the deeds of others. One moment, he was living in a family with a father who adored him, but his brothers actions turned his world upside down and there was nothing he could do about it.

As he was taken to Egypt, he must have wondered, *Will I ever see my father again? What will become of me? What did I do to deserve this treatment?*

The stage was set for depression and despair. Maybe you have felt these "bottomless pit" feelings. What did you do?

Sold as a common slave in Egypt, Joseph went from being the son of a wealthy man to the slave of a powerful man, Potiphar, the keeper of the guard for Pharaoh. Much like the Secret Service of our day, he protected the leader of the country. He was a man of wealth and obviously needed some additional help, so he bought Joseph. Potiphar had no idea how his life would be affected by the purchase of this Hebrew boy. Initially, Joseph served in the regular routine of slave boys. As time went by, Potiphar observed his character and recognized that Joseph was not your ordinary slave.

> Now his master saw that the Lord was with him and how the Lord caused all that he did to prosper in his hand. So Joseph found favor in his sight, and became his personal servant; and he made him overseer over his house, and all that he owned he put in his charge (Genesis 39:3, 4).

Even though Joseph was enslaved to another, he never acted like a slave. It was in the first stages of his journey that he realized his destiny. In examining Joseph's life, we can also search our own souls in times of crisis. What does it mean to walk with God in faith? Obviously it means far more than most of us realize. Joseph was forced to walk by faith, holding to the belief of God's higher purposes for his life. Author David Hazard calls this "the high road of faith." He draws this conclusion from reading the works of men like Oswald Chambers, Augustine, John of the Cross and other spiritual giants. In his work, "His Ways, Our Ways," he offers four foundational principles about the Biblical walk of faith. As I consider each, I see them lived out in young Joseph, especially when he worked in the house of Potiphar.

1. *God's view of life is higher than mine.* Stand on the creek bank and drop your line into the water. Listen to the birds and the babbling of the water flowing down to the ocean. Turn to the right and look down the stream as far as you can. Now turn to the left and see the water coming around the bend. Remember, that's all you can see. God's view is bigger.

Board an airplane and ask for a window seat. Watch as the plane takes off and rises into the clouds. On a clear day, even from 33,000 feet, you can see outlines of fields and the thread-like ribbons of highways. If you are observant, you can see for miles, but that is all. Only big things can be seen. God's view is so much broader— nothing escapes His view. He even sees the sparrow that dies and falls to the ground (see Matthew 6).

"Left to my own," Hazard writes, "I guess my way through based on how circumstances appear at any given moment . . . on whether the neurotransmitter channels in my brain are okay or in a depressive low." Joseph's life took another major turn. His schedule and activities were determined by someone who had no interest in him personally. He was stuck in a hopeless situation. What did Joseph do? He went about his job with peace and self-control, believing that God saw it all, had control of every situation and, in His perfect timing, would reveal His plan.

2. *God is never silent.* I get frustrated when I pray for a week about something and don't see any results. I need action and movement to maintain my resolve to keep praying. Long-term faith in a seemingly silent God is a spiritual struggle. My impatience does not move God, but He is there, no matter what happens.

> He's busy while you slumber. He's into the job while you're into your dreams. He's fully engaged when you've pulled the plug. The psalmist put it like this: "He who watches over you will not slumber; indeed, he who watches over Israel will neither slumber nor sleep" (Psalm 121:3, 4, *NIV*). This is the God who moves outside our vision and occupies Himself with tasks beyond our comprehension. His eyes peer into what we can't see and His hands work skillfully where we can only grope. This is the God who reaches and thinks and plans and shapes and watches and controls and feels and acts while we're unconscious under the sheet and a comforter. But don't get the idea that He's off attending to black holes and quasars or fussing with hydrogen molecules in some distant galaxy. God works the night shift for you. He's occupied all night long thinking about you. His interest in you never flags or diminishes. Not even for a heartbeat. He is busy on your behalf even when you are not aware of it, even when you are doing absolutely nothing. When it comes to your life, He never stops observing, giving, directing, guarding, and planning."[1]

Joseph contemplated his future and saw little chance for advancement. If he worked hard, he might work up to head slave and receive extra privileges. There was no chance in this world for the sun, the moon and 11 stars to bow to him as a slave to Potiphar! But while Joseph was serving faithfully, God was working on his future. A famine was coming, which no one knew about but God.

3. *God works in all circumstances.* The most impossible situations are God's best occasions for miracles. Nothing can intimidate Him. Shut the door on hope, drown your dreams in the bitter tears of disappointment—God will raise them to life. Raise the white flag of defeat, pretend it is all over, and watch God restore, renew and revitalize your life, ministry and purpose. It is God at work in the silent moments of your life that turn the pages of your spiritual history. When you thought it was over—it wasn't!

The Chinese bamboo tree has absolutely no growth for four years. However, in the fifth year, it shoots up in the air to enormous heights. The same can be true in the life of a believer. The devil has lied to some of you so long that you have begun to believe his account of your future. You may have quit trying and determined that the hurts are too many and the pain too much. The devil is a liar! If the story of Joseph teaches us anything, it is that the final chapter of your life has not yet been written. The finale is still to come. Disappointment and negative circumstances are real and must be survived, but God is preparing another set of circumstances for your life. Nothing that happens to you today will be in the final chapter. God has ordained your life for another dimension that only He controls—eternity! Listen to the prophet Jeremiah:

> For thus says the Lord, "When seventy years have been completed for Babylon, I will visit you and fulfill My

good word to you, to bring you back to this place. For I know the plans that I have for you," declares the Lord, "plans welfare and not for calamity to give you a future and a hope. Then you will call upon Me and come and pray to Me, and I will listen to you. And you will seek Me and find Me, when you search for Me with all your heart. And I will be found by you," declares the Lord, "and I will restore your fortunes and will gather you from all the nations and from all the places where I have driven you," declares the Lord, "and I will bring you back to the place from where I sent you into exile (Jeremiah 29:10-14).

It is never over until God says it is over!

4. *God's purposes are higher.* As I contemplate Joseph's struggles, I have to remind myself that he did not know what I know. I have read the end of the story. Joseph relied on his faith in God's higher purpose. Often, you and I get too bogged down in the present circumstances to appreciate God's ability to work beyond this moment. He prepares tomorrow with such a different backdrop than today—so marvelous and breathtaking that it makes us forget yesterday. That's what He did for Joseph. The moments of pain were lost in joy when God restored his family.[2]

Several things come to mind when observing Joseph's faithfulness.

THE DILEMMA

Like you and me, Joseph was a young man with a destiny. God's grace was so evident in his life that even Potiphar noticed it.

We can learn from Scripture that if we live in full obedience to God, we are examples to those who interact
with us every day. This is the message of Matthew 5: "You
are the light of the world. A city set on a hill cannot be hidden. Nor do men light a lamp, and put it under the peck-
measure, but on the lampstand; and it gives light to all
who are in the house. Let your light shine before men in
such a way that they may see your good works, and glo-
rify your Father who is in heaven" (vv. 14-16). You and I
can also influence others when we allow God to work in
and through us.

> We have a tendency to look for wonder in our experi-
> ence, and we mistake heroic actions for real heroes. It's
> one thing to go through a crisis grandly, yet quite anoth-
> er to go through every day glorifying God when there is
> no witness, no limelight, and no one paying even the
> remotest attention to us. If we are not looking for halos,
> we at least want something that will make people say,
> "What a wonderful man of prayer he is!" or, "What a
> great woman of devotion she is!" If you are properly
> devoted to the Lord Jesus, you have reached the lofty
> height where no one would ever notice you personally.
> All that is noticed is the power of God coming through
> you all the time. . . . To do even the most humbling tasks
> to the glory of God takes the Almighty God Incarnate
> working in us. . . . The true test of a saint's life is not suc-
> cessfulness but faithfulness on the human level of life.
> We tend to set up success in Christian work as our pur-
> pose, but our purpose should be to display the glory of
> God in human life, to live a life "hidden with Christ in
> God" in our everyday human conditions (Colossians
> 3:3). Our human relationships are the very conditions in
> which the ideal life of God should be exhibited.[3]

53

I imagine Potiphar had seen scores of religious people. They came and went from Pharaoh's palace frequently, attempting to gain favor with the leadership. Their goals were to maneuver the political system for their own personal agenda. As such they maligned the name of God because they attempted to use their relationship with God for their own benefit. Potiphar was not impressed with them. Joseph was different—he had no agenda. He could not change his situation as a slave, yet he was consistent in his everyday life. This intrigued his master. He trusted Joseph.

Joseph did not allow the tremendous weight of his life's circumstances to overwhelm him to the point of despair. We all are susceptible at times. The crushing weight of stress and negative events can almost tip over our boat. Unless we stay focused on God and His enabling strength, we would quit.

When Paul was sailing toward Rome, a ferocious storm came. The situation appeared to be hopeless. The sailors began to prepare to escape when Paul warned them, "Unless these men remain in the ship, you yourselves cannot be saved" (Acts 27:31).

At times, when I am about to lower the life raft, I can almost hear the warning from the Lord: Don't abandon ship! God has promised us a safe landing. The ride may be bumpy and we may get some salt in our faces, but we will land safely. Despite all that was going on around Joseph, he remained faithful to his employer, his dreams and his God. We must do the same.

BETTER OR BITTER

Joseph had every reason to be bitter and discouraged. He could have been angry and no one would have wondered why. His life and dreams had been stripped from him without just cause. Yet, in slavery, far from home, Joseph was faithfully living out his life in obedience to his God, and God was making his life something valuable.

Joseph never adopted the "victim mentality" that is so prevalent today. We are so quick to look for someone or something other than ourselves to blame. Then we see ourselves as victims, to the point of the complete collapse of our dreams and desires.

Wayne Dyer writes:

All blame is a waste of time. No matter how much fault you find with another, and regardless of how much you blame him, it will not change you. The only thing blame does is to keep the focus off you when you are looking for external reasons to explain your unhappiness or frustration. You may succeed in making another feel guilty about something by blaming him, but you won't succeed in changing whatever it is about you that is making you unhappy.[4]

Joseph did not lament over where he would be if his jealous brothers had not tried to ruin his life. At this point, he did what he could—he committed it to God and continued to be faithful.

Jim Cymbala and his wife, Carol, pastor the Brooklyn Tabernacle Church in New York City. In his book, *Fresh*

Wind, Fresh Fire, he addresses this victim mentality of our society.

> When you work in the inner city, as I do, the victim mentality can be very strong. "I'm black, or brown, so it's hard for me to get anywhere in life. I was molested as a child by my uncle, and I'm still dealing with the pain of that." I often reply, "Yes, those things are real—but God is greater. None of us can afford to blame the past indefinitely."[5]

An interesting story is told in John 5 about a lame man who sat by a pool that was visited in certain seasons by an angel. Many sick people were placed beside the pool to wait for the waters to be troubled so they could get in first and be healed. One particular man lay there for 38 years. No doubt, he had become a victim of those who forsook him—his family, friends and bystanders, who did not help him to get in the water quickly enough to be healed. The despair and disillusionment of his plight can be heard in his response to the Lord's inquiry, "Do you wish to get well?" Listen to this victim's reply: "Sir, I have no man to put me into the pool when the water is stirred up, but while I am coming, another steps down before me " (John 5:7).

Listen carefully to a man who had been abandoned. Does he want to be healed? You bet. But no one helps him. His state was the fault of others who had abandoned him in his critical time of need. Sound familiar? Most of us are guilty. We quickly blame others for what has happened. In time, we begin to believe our lack of progress has been the fault of others. If you are looking to blame someone else, you are the loser. The sooner you realize this, the sooner things will change. Joseph refused to blame others. Even in the end, he was determined not to blame his brothers or seek revenge. He understood that God takes care of His children, in spite of the action of others. Your resource is not some man or an organization—it is God! And His record is remarkable.

JOSEPH REFUSED TO LET THE PAST DEFINE THE PRESENT

Joseph recognized that those who wronged him could change his circumstances and his environment, but they could never change his heart. He could not help what his brothers did, what his employer said or what his so-called friends did. He chose to follow his heart after God and be at peace about life.

There are few things that impress God more than faithfulness. More than 100 times He refers to faithfulness and faithful men or women on whom He depended. He seeks out such people. "But I will raise up for Myself a faithful priest who will do according to what is in My heart and in My soul; and I will build him an enduring house, and he will walk before My anointed always" (1 Samuel 2:35). "A faithful man will abound with blessings, but he who makes haste to be rich will not go unpunished" (Proverbs 28:20). It should not surprise us that God blessed Joseph and his work.

Joseph's mind was settled on God and in His providence. When you and I take that posture in life, God can make a prison a place of blessing. He can make the atmosphere of the most oppressive marriage and home life a place of blessing and anointing. How can we know for sure? "When a man's ways are pleasing to the Lord, he makes even his enemies to be at peace with him"

(Proverbs 16:7). God was at work and, though Potiphar did not realize it, he was part of the plan to bring Joseph to the place of God's appointment. So, as Potiphar's confidence in Joseph expanded, he made Joseph his personal servant. That's some promotion for a young man with no credentials.

Some life applications seem evident at this point in the story. I share them in hopes they strengthen you to be what God has appointed you to be.

Negative circumstances do not have the power to change our outlook on life. The ability to pick up broken pieces of disappointment in life and continue to move forward is impressive. When most people get knocked down, they moan and groan and throw a pity party. They question God, the Bible and other people of faith. They linger too long at the point of hurt and are adversely affected by life's disappointing moments. This is not to imply any lack of compassion for those of us who have been wounded by situations that hurt us deeply. However, it is important not to linger too long. Take time to reflect, adjust and then move on. The Enemy's plan is to chain you to the disappointment in your life so you will never be what God intends. The choice is yours. God offers the beautiful opportunity to step from that negative experience and find a fresh anointing for the next day.

Joseph could have taken the attitude that he didn't care about Potiphar's house. He had been hurt and no one was helping him, so why should he care about anyone else? Instead, he surrendered his hurts to God, committed his future to Him and continued being the best servant he could be for Potiphar. He treated his master and his property with respect and caught the attention of Potiphar with his work ethic and attitude. Even an unbeliever could not help noticing what an exceptional young man Joseph was. Whether he knew the history behind Joseph's experience, we do not know. But Potiphar was impressed.

> So it was, from the time that he had made him overseer of his house and all that he had, that the Lord blessed the Egyptian's house for Joseph's sake; and the blessing of the Lord was on all that he had in the house and in the field (Genesis 39:5, NKJV).

Proper humility of my heart keeps everything going in the right direction. I recently read this definition of humility: "Humility is thinking true, realistic thoughts about God and ourselves."[6] Somewhere in Joseph's past there was a teacher who instilled in his heart a right attitude toward God. Perhaps it was his father, but someone did a great job teaching Joseph about God. In all of his adjustments to new circumstances, Joseph saw God as the director and controller of all. Good or bad, God was in control. There was a perceived peace of mind that dominated Joseph's life. It is the simple assurance of divine protection and assistance. God does that for the humble. "Therefore it says, 'God is opposed the proud, but gives grace to the humble.' . . . Be miserable and mourn and weep; let your laughter be turned into mourning, and your joy to gloom. Humble yourselves in the presence of the Lord, and He will exalt you" (James 4:6, 9, 10). "The Lord supports the afflicted; He brings down the wicked to the ground" (Psalm 147:6). "Even to your old age, I shall be the same, and even to your graying years I shall bear you! I have done it, and I shall carry you; and I shall bear you, and I shall deliver you" (Isaiah 46:4).

Regardless of who is responsible, life has its moments of disappointment and frustration. The process God sends us through is not always the one we like. When Peter wrote to the early church, he reminded them, "In this you greatly rejoice, even though now for a little while, if necessary, you have been distressed by various trials" (1 Peter 1:6).

When we have questions that seem to have no answers, we trust that God knows the way to our completeness in Him. While His ways are not easily understood, they are the best for us. Joseph had that insight. Life was not good and he was far from home. He must have wondered how things were back in Canaan. He thought of his father and missed him. The turns his life had taken had a reason and a cause. The end product was the fulfillment of all God had promised. In Joseph's story, you and I recognize the truth of Paul's words, "For I consider that the sufferings of this present time are not worthy to be compared with the glory that is to be revealed to us" (Romans 8:18). No matter what it takes, or how it plays out, God is committed to our salvation and He is conforming us to the image of His Son, Jesus Christ. So don't grow weary of the process. Keep the end in sight and know it won't rain always.

In a revival meeting in Alabama, I finished preaching about the power of forgiveness in Joseph's life. On the way to my car, a man overwrought with emotion, grabbed me and said, "Your message today about Joseph was right on track. I only wish I had heard it 15 years ago. Now I ask you—what do I do now that I have completely messed up my life with irrevocable mistakes?"

It is a common question when considering a life filled with mistakes that have brought dire consequences. There is really only one thing to do—it is what Joseph did. He simply entrusted his life and all that he had to deal with to God, knowing He is "able to do exceeding abundantly beyond all that we ask or think" (Ephesians 3:20).

Some things cannot be changed and we are left to deal with painful consequences. No one promised us a life without disappointment. We do not know what the coming days hold. Yet, we know God is faithful and He will bring peace of mind according to His power and grace. We hope for days that are not marked by tragedy and reversals, but if they come, we know that our lives are in His hands and He will not forsake us.

The following quote by Andrew Murray sums up this feeling that belongs to God's children:

> Humility is perfect quietness of heart . . . never to be irritated or sore or disappointed. It is to expect nothing, to wonder at nothing that is done to me. . . . It is best to be at rest when nobody praises me and when I am blamed or despised. It is to have a blessed home in the Lord where I can go and shut the door and kneel to my Father in secret and be at peace as in a deep sea of calmness when all around me is trouble.
>
> –Andrew Murray

*A*nd it came about after these events that his master's wife looked with desire at Joseph, and she said, "Lie with me." But he refused and said to his master's wife, "Behold, with me here, my master does not concern himself with anything in the house, and he has put all that he owns in my charge. There is no one greater in this house than I, and he has withheld nothing from me except you, because you are his wife. How then could I do this great evil, and sin against God?" And it came about as she spoke to Joseph day after day, that he did not listen to her, to lie beside her, or be with her.

Genesis 39:7-10

CHAPTER FOUR

When You Are in the Heat of Temptation

Have you ever noticed that your most vulnerable moments are not when you are distressed or attacked by the enemy? In moments like these we are probably closest to God, because we are praying and fasting, seeking the Lord for help.

Rather, I believe our most vulnerable moments are those that come after our greatest victories when we are blessed and feeling comfortable. Why? Maybe because we are not alert during these times.

- In 1 Kings 18, Elijah had just defeated 450 of Baal's prophets and publicly humiliated King Ahab and those who opposed Jehovah God. What a triumph! Only moments later, he was in the throes of depression and despondency because of the threat of one woman—Queen Jezebel. It seems incredible that someone who had accomplished so much would be afraid so quickly, but it proves my point.

- In 2 Samuel 11, after King David had established Israel as a mighty nation and established peace, he was vulnerable. Unalert, he succumbed to weakness of the flesh and committed a horrible sin with Bathsheba that resulted in murder, deception and devastation. This did not occur when he was running from King Saul. In the days when he was threatened, he sang to the Lord, wrote psalms and communed with God daily. He had been lean and strong, but he became fat, lazy and vulnerable.

- Ananias and Sapphira were part of a powerful Pentecostal church experiencing revival in Acts 2—4. As part of their unity and faith, the church agreed to sell their earthly possessions and pool the funds to help the poor. Everyone agreed. This couple, of whom we know very little, promised to sell their property. In a weak moment, they held back some money and lied about the amount they received for the land. Right in the middle of a great move of God, they became vulnerable to failure (see Acts 5).

People often discover too late that their vulnerability is evident in the most unexpected times. Listen to the advice of the apostle Paul: "Therefore let him who thinks he stands take heed lest he fall" (1 Corinthians 10:12).

Joseph made the journey to Egypt after having been sold by his own brothers to Ishmaelite traders. A wealthy man named Potiphar purchased Joseph and made him a servant in his household. Potiphar was the captain of the guard, an Egyptian officer of Pharaoh. His job was protecting the nation's leader, a man of influence and power. Joseph's talents and abilities did not go unnoticed by Potiphar. He made Joseph the overseer of his house and its operations. Good things happened for Joseph because God's hand was upon his life. Even Potiphar's household was blessed of God because of Joseph. Then the trouble began.

Potiphar's wife was attracted to Joseph and began to work a plan of enticement. But Joseph refused her offer. She continued to invite him to commit sexual sin with her, but each time he resisted. His answer to her gives us an insight into his heart (see Genesis 39:7-9).

POTIPHAR'S TRUST

Joseph did not take lightly the trust Potiphar extended to him. Everything Potiphar had was in Joseph's care, except his wife. That's how much his employer trusted him. Joseph was serious about his commitment to his employer. Some would say that Joseph should not have cared about Potiphar's belongings, since he was only a slave, held against his will. But Joseph saw himself as a man who had an appointment with destiny. Every decision weighed against the desire of remaining true to God. Furthermore, there is something to be said about a work ethic that respects those who have given you responsibility. The apostles Paul and Peter address this issue several times in the New Testament.

Slaves, be obedient to those who are your masters according to the flesh, with fear and trembling, in the sincerity of your heart, as to Christ; not by way of eyeservice, as men-pleasers, but as slaves of Christ, doing the will of God from the heart. With good will render service, as to the Lord, and not to men, knowing that whatever good thing each one does, this he will receive back from the Lord, whether slave or free (Ephesians 6:5-8).

Servants, be submissive to your masters with all respect, not only to those who are good and gentle, but also to those who are unreasonable. For this finds favor, if for the sake of conscience toward God a man bears up under sorrows when suffering unjustly. For what credit is there if, when you sin and are harshly treated, you endure it with patience? But if when you do what is right and suffer for it you patiently endure it, this finds favor with God. For you have been called to this purpose, since Christ also suffered for you, leaving you an example for you to follow in His steps (1 Peter 2:18-21).

Joseph's behavior and work ethic made an impression on Potiphar. He had worked hard to gain the trust of this man. As such, he was not willing to cash all of that good-will in for something so fleeting. Our reputation and relationship with others are not to be taken lightly. In this day, it seems that the more sordid the past and the more immoral someone becomes, the greater the degree of notoriety. However, these people betray themselves. One day, they will realize they have sacrificed too much.

HIS RELATIONSHIP WITH GOD

Forget the fact that it was wrong to do this to the man who trusted him, Joseph had a more powerful and higher purpose for rejecting the advances of Potiphar's wife. His relationship with his God was more important to him than she could comprehend. To compromise would have been in direct conflict with what God wanted for him.

I believe Joseph saw this temptation for what it was— a detour. If Mrs. Potiphar had been successful in her attempts to seduce young Joseph, his destiny would have been forfeited. Let's imagine for a moment a scenario where Mrs. Potiphar can promise advancement and approval from her husband if he just plays her game. Joseph sees this as an acceptable notion and concedes to her wish. Can he be forgiven? Of course, but his sexual sin puts him in direct conflict with God's law.

God's forgiveness is promised to those who seek it, but there are consequences of sin. She will get tired of him eventually and trade him for someone else. Individuals like Mrs. Potiphar see people like Joseph as disposable toys to play with and throw away when they are done. Furthermore, to violate his principles will further deteriorate his self-respect.

Our enemy is Satan. The apostle Paul describes our battle with him in this manner:

> For our struggle is not against flesh and blood, but against the rulers, against the powers, against the world forces of this darkness, against the spiritual forces of wickedness in the heavenly places (Ephesians 6:12).

The Enemy attempts to deceive us and provoke us to sin against God. As we determine to fight the good fight of faith against the flesh, we can be certain Satan will do everything he can to hinder us. A couple of reminders about our Enemy might be helpful to someone who is fighting temptation.

In his beginning, Satan was an angel of God. Because of his evil pride and desire to take God's place, he was dismissed from heaven and fell to earth. Jesus said, "I was watching Satan fall from heaven like lightning" (Luke 10:18). When he was thrown out of heaven, a portion of the angels were cast out with him. They make up the consortium of evil spirits and demons who promote wickedness among God's creation. For a season of time, determined by God, these evil spirits/fallen angels will work in this world. However, remember a couple of important things:

1. *Satan is only an angel.* He only has the power of an angel. Unfortunately, some believe he is equal with God in power and authority. As an angel, he is still restricted to the abilities of an angel. Our God is omniscient (all-knowing). He knows what you are thinking right now—Satan does not. He cannot read your mind. What he knows about you is basically limited to two things—what you tell him and what you show him. Because his knowledge of you is limited, he and his cohorts strategically study you and analyze what you do, how you act and react, so that they can develop a plan to attack you. Attacks against your spiritual walk with God are not random or accidental. Your Enemy does an excellent job of noticing where you are vulnerable. He will exploit you in any way he can contrive. This is the reason we are admonished to be alert to Satan's devices.

2. *Satan operates under the authority of God.* The Bible makes it crystal clear: "There is no authority except from God" (Romans 13:1). Not only does God restrict the time Satan can work in this world, but God also determines

to what extent he can work against His children. Satan needed God's permission to attack Job. Only when God temporarily removed His protection was Satan able to do anything to harm Job.

The admonition of Scripture is for us to be alert, on guard against any attempt by the Enemy to succeed. He will find your vulnerabilities. Don't place yourself in a position where Satan can gain any advantage over you.

Satan's attempts to deter you will be subtle and deceptive, because his goal is to keep you from fellowship with God. He knows God has touched your life and that He has a destiny for you. Satan wants to keep you from reaching it. Thankfully, Joseph was not willing to trade his destiny for a one-night stand!

The subtleties of sin are tools of Satan. Very seldom does the Enemy deal with us directly. Remember, he caused Eve to rationalize sin and ignore the potential consequences. After the fact, it was too late to realize how deadly her decision was for all humanity. In far too many cases, we fail to see the consequences—we are blinded by the potential pleasures and personal happiness we think such actions or deeds will bring.

For many years, advertisers gave the impression that smoking was the cool thing to do. Tall cowboys smoking cigarettes astride huge powerful horses were seen as symbols of manhood. Many people were deceived by this image, not realizing that it carried side effects of pain, despair and death. The coughing patients dying of lung cancer were never used in advertisements.

Few people think about the consequences of sin. Satan does not want such a thought process to take place,so he attempts to get you to make quick decisions. My wife, Kathy, and I have often wished that those who are tempted to violate their marriage and family vows would pause long enough to count the cost for their children, family and reputation. Seldom does that occur. The price of sin is high, and the victims are many. Those who play with fire will be burned.

It might be helpful to consider the consequences of sin when faced with temptation. Many would change their minds if they considered the outcome. In his article, "Consequences of a Moral Tumble," Randy Alcorn says that whenever he is feeling "particularly vulnerable to sexual temptation," he finds it helpful to review the effects such actions could have:

- Grieving my Redeemer

- One day having to look Jesus in the face and give an account of my actions

- Inflicting untold hurt on my best friend and loyal wife, and losing her respect and trust

- Hurting my beloved daughters

- Destroying my example and credibility with my children, and nullifying both present and future efforts to teach them to obey God

- Bringing shame to my family

- Creating a form of guilt awfully hard to shake; even though God could forgive me, could I forgive myself?

- Forming memories and flashbacks that could plague future intimacy with my wife

- Wasting years of ministry training and experience

- Undermining the faithful example and hard work of other Christians in our community

- Bringing pleasure to Satan, the enemy of God and good

- Possibly bearing the physical consequences of sexually transmitted diseases; possibly infecting my wife

- Possibly causing pregnancy, with its personal and financial implications

- Causing shame and hurt to my friends, especially those I've led to Christ and discipled.[1]

What a sobering list! You and I must never forget what I believe Joseph considered—there are consequences to sin, even though God forgives.

If you commit a violent crime with a handgun, and are honestly and sincerely sorry for your sin, you can be assured of God's full and complete forgiveness—but the penalties will still impact your life. The forgiveness of God is abundant, but the consequences of sin are real.

> Do not be deceived, God is not mocked; for whatever a man sows, this will he also reap. For the one who sows to his own flesh shall from the flesh reap corruption, but the one who sows to the Spirit shall from the Spirit reap eternal life (Galatians 6:7, 8).

Joseph determined correctly that no amount of pleasure would be worth the potential he would face if he accepted Mrs. Potiphar's offer. Like Moses, Joseph was forced to choose a less appealing road in order to ensure a greater future.

One of my concerns as it relates to young people in our churches is the perceived casualness with which some approach the forgiveness of God. They ignore the consequences of their actions. Dr. Paul Conn, president of Lee University, once stated, "Our children have the physical capacity to destroy themselves before they possess the maturity to understand the consequences of their actions."

Even the devil will use the grace of God to push you to do things that violate your relationship with God. Grace is not cheap and God is not obligated to simply bail you out. In case you are wondering, the voice that whispers, "Go ahead—you can always ask God to forgive you later!" is not the voice of God or His Spirit.

Joseph's virtue in resisting the solicitations of his mistress was truly exemplary. Had he reasoned after the manner of men, he might have soon found that the proposed intrigue might be carried on with the utmost secrecy and greatly to his secular advantage. But he chose to risk all rather than injure a kind benefactor, defile his conscience, and sin against God. Such conduct is so exceedingly rare that his example has stood on the records of time as almost without a parallel, admired by all, applauded by most, and in similar circumstances, I am afraid, imitated by few. The fable of the brave and virtuous Bellerophon and Stheneboea, wife of Proetus, king of the Argives, was probably founded on this history. Joseph fled and got him out. To know when to fight and when to fly are of great importance in the Christian life. Some temptations must be manfully met, resisted, and thus overcome; from others we must fly. He who stands to contend or reason, especially in such case as that mentioned here, is infallibly ruined. Principiis obsta, "resist the first overtures of sin," is a good maxim. After-remedies come too late (*Clarke's Commentary*).

This was a pivotal moment in young Joseph's life. His destiny and relationship with God was hanging in the balance, but he passed the test with flying colors. These reminders keep me aware of how crafty the Enemy is in his attempts to destroy me.

This challenge came at a time in Joseph's life when things were beginning to improve for him. A careful reading of the preceding verses leaves the impression that things were improving for Joseph. It wasn't home, but God was blessing him and he was beginning to get on with his life, albeit away from his family and home. Temptations always come at unusual times. Satan seems to sense the right moment to attack. He waits for times when we are most vulnerable, and then he moves in. We are admonished to be alert to his attacks. Peter advises: "Be of sober spirit, be on the alert. Your adversary, the devil, prowls about like a roaring lion, seeking someone to devour" (1 Peter 5:8). We are not ignorant of what Satan is doing. Stay alert!

The challenge was constantly before Joseph, causing him to deal with it daily. It is one thing to deal with a single temptation, but she never quit. She heard "No," but she would not accept it! Don't you imagine Joseph began to dread each day and her inevitable advances? He must have tried to avoid her all day, every day.

The decision to resist was personal and brought adversity into his life; it ultimately brought Joseph to a place of new opportunity for service to the Lord. You can be sure this was not an easy decision for Joseph. He was in a strange land, cut off from his family support. The Enemy must have said to Joseph, "No one will ever know—enjoy yourself!" Joseph knew better. So he made the choice, knowing it might affect his position in the household. The boss's wife had an unusual and powerful influence on the boss. If she wanted to get rid of him, she could, yet there was peace in Joseph's heart. He knew that making the right decision would pay off in the end.

So how did it come out in the end? You may think that, like the dramas on television, Mrs. Potiphar was found out, Joseph was vindicated and hailed as a hero. This was not the case.

One day, after making sure everyone was out of the house, she made a bold attempt to force Joseph to commit sexual sin with her. She grabbed him by his coat and demanded that he obey her wishes. He resisted and fled, leaving his coat in her hand. Joseph's actions were aligned with the advice the apostle Paul would give, centuries later: "Flee immorality. Every other sin that a man commits is outside the body, but the immoral man sins against his own body" (1 Corinthians 6:18).

Joseph was defenseless against her accusations. She reported that he had tried to rape her. Her personal embarrassment at his rebuff would not permit her to admit the truth—he was able to resist her. She concocted a more palatable story: the Hebrew slave had made an unwanted advance and, when she screamed in terror, he fled, leaving his coat as evidence. Joseph was ruined. Potiphar was furious and prepared to punish Joseph. As a slave, Joseph had no legal standing to defend himself against her accusations. Before Potiphar, it was simply his wife's story against Joseph's. Potiphar's wife related her story to the other servants, not giving Joseph an opportunity to tell his side of the story and effectively cutting him off from any peer support.

Adam Clarke writes:

> A woman of the spirit of Potiphar's wife is capable of any species of evil. When she could not get her wicked ends answered, she began to accuse. This is precisely Satan's custom: he first tempts men to sin, and then accuses them as having committed it, even where the temptation has been faithfully and perseveringly resisted! By this means he can trouble a tender conscience, and weaken faith by bringing confusion into the mind. Thus the inexperienced especially are often distracted and cast down; hence Satan is properly called the accuser of the brethren, Revelation 12:10 (*Clarke's Commentary*, Genesis 39).

When Potiphar heard his wife's story, he was extremely angry. Joseph was placed in a jail where the king's prisoners were kept. It certainly was not fair, but even in jail, God kept His hand upon Joseph. The Scripture says regarding his stay in prison: "And he was there in the jail. But the Lord was with Joseph and extended kindness to him, and gave him favor in the sight of the chief jailer" (Genesis 39:20, 21).

Even in prison, God was watching over His servant. There is no situation where God cannot care for His children. Whether in prison, a fiery furnace, a lion's den or a hostile home, God is in control of your life and, as He did for Joseph, God will make sure you are all right.

There is a familiar verse of Scripture dealing with temptation, which I believe each of us should commit to memory. It is sound advice to each of us, especially when temptation comes:

> No temptation has overtaken you but such as is common to man; and God is faithful, who will not allow you to be tempted beyond what you are able, but with the temptation will provide the way of escape also, that you may be able to endure it (1 Corinthians 10:13).

Everyone has temptation. What tempts one does not necessarily tempt another. For me personally, I can honestly say I have never been tempted to drink alcohol. You could "pop the top" on a can of Milwaukee's finest, leave it right under my nose, and I promise you, I would not be tempted. Yet, there are others who cannot resist the draw of alcohol. Paul wants us to realize that temptation will certainly come. Be prepared and don't think that you have been singled out for adversity.

God is faithful. When the heat is on, according to Paul, you can count on God for at least two things:

1. *You will never be tempted beyond your ability to cope.* Sometimes we think that what we are facing is impossible to conquer, but God promises that we will not have to deal with more than we are able to stand. Regardless of what we encounter, God has confidence in our ability

to survive or He would not allow it. Remember when Job was being tempted by Satan, God put restrictions and limits on what Satan was permitted to do. God, who is so intimately involved with you, knows your limits. He is faithful to keep His promise and watch your load limits.

2. *God will make sure you make it. The Living Bible* renders the last part of the verse: "He will show you how to escape temptation's power so that you bear up patiently against it" (1 Corinthians 10:13). That is just like the Lord. When Kathy was a little girl, her older brother would wait outside the school for her, alert for any danger that might come her way. If some bully started to harass her, it was her brother who would step out in the open and make his presence known. That's like my God! He is just around the corner, watching the whole thing you are dealing with and making sure you are OK. He is ready to step in and take matters into His hands, should you need help. He is committed to your survival.

Remember, God had a plan for Joseph, and He was committed to it. Given Joseph's resolve to follow the Lord's way, you can be sure God would not allow a lustful woman or an angry master to circumvent His plan.

If you are a person of purpose, pursuing God, you can count on the Enemy to throw difficult obstacles into your path to detour you from your pursuit of God. Life will have its temptations, but we just have to stand strong and trust God.

One of the lessons the life of Joseph teaches is that all temptation can be overcome, and adversity need not short-circuit our dreams. We can stand tall in the face of Satan's attack, knowing God is our helper. Our future is secure in Him!

*S*o Joseph's master took him and put him into
the jail, the place where the king's prisoners
were confined; and he was there in the jail.
But the Lord was with Joseph and extended
kindness to him, and gave him favor in the sight
of the chief jailer. And the chief jailer committed
to Joseph's charge all the prisoners who were
in the jail; so that whatever was done there, he
was responsible for it. The chief jailer did
not supervise anything under Joseph's
charge because the Lord was with him; and
whatever he did, the Lord made to prosper. . . .
Then Joseph said to him, "This is the inter-
pretation of it: the three branches are three
days; within three more days Pharaoh will
lift up your head and restore you to your office;
and you will put Pharaoh's cup into his
hand according to your former custom when
you were his cupbearer. Only keep me in mind
when it goes well with you, and please do
me a kindness by mentioning me to Pharaoh,
and get me out of this house. For I was in
fact kidnapped from the land of the Hebrews,
and even here I have done nothing that they
should have put me into the dungeon."
Genesis 39:20-23; 40:12-15

CHAPTER FIVE

WHEN THOSE YOU HELP DON'T REMEMBER

Those you help the most will forget you the quickest!" Have you found this to be true in your life? The people whom you make the greatest effort to help will often be the ones who later try to stone you. My dad and mom have been pastors in North Carolina for more than 35 years.

Over the years, I have observed that the people my parents tried to help the most were the very ones who gave them the most grief in their churches. It seems incredible that those who have enjoyed the benefits seem the quickest to forget and turn on those who bless them. Some of us have unbelievably short memories.

It hardly seems possible that Joseph could have encountered more adversity, given the bizarre and unusual way his life had gone up to this point, but he did! He was in jail, accused of trying to sexually assault the wife of a rich and powerful officer in Pharaoh's court. Some scholars speculate Potiphar may not have fully believed his wife's story, or he would have had Joseph killed. But to publicly support his wife and save face, he had Joseph imprisoned in a dungeon, where his roommates were the criminals of society. This was not the kind of place for a young man whose life was under divine appointment.

God often places His servants in some of life's most difficult situations. During my first pastorate, I read a quote in the newspaper that stated: "Christians are like tea bags—they are no good unless they have been in some hot water!" In the fiery furnace, our true self is revealed. In his classic book, *The Gulag Archipelago*, Aleksandr Solzhenitsyn writes concerning his imprisonment:

> In the intoxication of youthful successes I had felt myself to be infallible, and I was therefore cruel. In the surfeit of power I was a murderer, and an oppressor. In my most evil moments I was convinced I was doing good, and I was well supplied with systematic arguments. And it was only when I lay there on rotting prison straw that I sensed within myself the first stirring of good. Gradually, it was disclosed to me that the line separating good and evil passes not through states, not between classes, nor between political parties either—but right through every human heart—and through all human hearts. . . . So bless you, prison, for having been in my life.[1]

The words of Andrae Crouch's song, "Through It All," approprietally describes the feelings of many. If we never had any problems, how could we know God could solve them? We couldn't.

Recently, I read with great interest the apology of Jim Bakker regarding his imprisonment from charges relating to his leadership of the PTL ministry. Mr. Bakker stated that his prison experience revealed God for who He is and helped him strip away the facade with which he had deceived himself and others. It is doubtful he would have come to such a life-changing revelation had he not experienced adversity.

Our greatest lessons are learned from our struggles and not from our achievement. At least, it seems so in my own life. Malcolm Muggeridge said:

> Contrary to what might be expected, I look back on experiences that at the time seemed especially desolating and painful, with particular satisfaction. Indeed I can say with complete truthfulness that everything I have learned in my seventy-five years in this world, everything that has truly enhanced and enlightened my existence, has been through affliction and not through happiness, whether pursued or attained. In other words, if it were to be possible to eliminate affliction from our earthly existence by means of some drug or other medical mumbo jumbo, . . . the result would not be to make life delectable, but to make it too banal and trivial to be endurable. This of course is what the Cross signifies. And it is the Cross more than anything else, that has called me inexorably to Christ.[2]

Joseph's imprisonment again caused him to take a deep look within and determine his course. In light of today's "feel-good, God-loves-you culture," he could have . . .

- become discouraged and lonely

- assumed falsely that God's plan was not going to work out

- counted himself a victim of his mother's death, his father's passivity and his brothers' hatred.

All of these would have qualified him for the talk show circuit where he could moan and complain about how mistreated he was. But not Joseph. Reading his story, you sense that although he was buffeted, he was not moved. There is not one hint of anger, bitterness or resentment—just faithfulness to God and adjustment to his surroundings. Interestingly, he does not seem to accept the wrongs done to him as personal, but he sees God's hand at work in everything.

How many times have we quoted the following verse to offer encouragement to someone who has suffered loss or misfortune? "And we know God causes all things to work together for good to those who love God, to those who are called according to His purpose" (Romans 8:28).

Do we really understand what the verse means? Unfortunately, in many cases I don't think we do, because not everything that happens to us is good. We may have unexpected death in our families, loss of jobs or sicknesses in our bodies.

The principle of this verse emphasizes God's ability to take all that occurs in our lives, both good and bad, and work out a marvelous plan that glorifies Him and the kingdom of God. Points of adversity that cause us pain can serve as places God can reveal His power and glory.

They can be starting points for a deeper and closer walk with Him.

For those of us who love the Lord, whose devotion and commitment to God is rooted in our soul, we should remember that God is committed to our soul's salvation. He orders our steps and works everything according to His sovereign will. Rather than discourage Joseph, it seems his trials and adversity drove him to a closer, more committed walk with the Lord. After all, it was all he really had.

THE LORD WAS WITH JOSEPH

"But the Lord was with Joseph and extended kindness to him, and gave him favor in the sight of the chief jailer" (Genesis 39:21). There are two references (vv. 21, 23) that remind us Joseph was not alone in that prison.

> We can all see God in exceptional things, but it requires the growth of spiritual discipline to see God in every detail. Never believe that the so-called random events of life are anything less than God's appointed order. Be ready to discover His divine designs anywhere and everywhere.[3]

There were prisoners of every sort there—murderers, rapists, thieves, and so on. Yet, even in that environment, God was there with Joseph. You and I can be comforted to know regardless of where we are—in prison or otherwise—God's abiding presence is with us. His presence is not restricted by those whose intent is evil or wicked. God's presence is always with us. It is a Biblical theme found throughout the Scripture:

- When the children of Israel were threatened by Pharaoh's army, God's visible presence was seen in the pillar of fire.

- When the three Hebrew children were thrown into a fiery furnace because they would not worship false idol gods, God's presence was with them in the form of a fourth man in the fire, visible to the king.

- When Daniel spent a night in the lion's den, he told King Darius the next morning, "O king, live forever! My God sent His angel and shut the lions' mouths, and they have not harmed me, inasmuch as I was found innocent before Him; and also toward you, O king, I have committed no crime" (Daniel 6:21, 22).

The list is too lengthy to provide every example; however, the principle is true—God's presence never leaves us. He is especially visible in our most desperate moments. Peter encouraged the weary saints in Asia Minor with these words: "Though you have not seen Him, you love Him, and though you do not see Him now, but believe in Him, you greatly rejoice with joy inexpressible and full of glory" (1 Peter 1:8).

The writer of Hebrews said: "He Himself has said, 'I will never desert you, nor will I forsake you,' so that we confidently say, 'The Lord is my helper, I will not be afraid. What shall man do to me?'" (Hebrews 13:5, 6). Such verses give us confidence of God's abiding presence in times of distress and trouble. In our lives, Kathy and I have been witnesses to the abiding presence of God:

- When our babies were sick during the night and everyone was asleep, there was an abiding presence of God that comforted us when Kathy and I prayed for them.

- When Kathy's father underwent two open-heart surgeries, God was there.

- When my grandfather passed away after I spent the last night with him in a hospital room, the Holy Spirit comforted me.

In 1990, while I lived in Lexington, Kentucky, I received a distressing call from my grandmother. She and my grandfather had been traveling by car from Colorado to my house. They had stopped at a motel in Illinois for the night. Unloading the car, my grandfather collapsed. Before medical help arrived, he died. Now, my aged grandmother was all alone in a motel, far from home and family, with no one to help. Fortunately, a wonderful Church of God pastor and his wife went to her at my request and stayed with her until I could get there. I found her sitting in a chair in the room, quite shocked, but alert. For hours, she had been comforted by the presence of God and His angels, who enabled her to stay calm in this time of distress.

So it was with Joseph. This unforeseen turn in Joseph's road led him to an awful prison where God's hand was still able to move. The Bible says, "The Lord was with Joseph and extended kindness to him, and gave him favor in the sight of the chief jailer" (Genesis 39:21). That's God!

As a group, jailers are suspicious. Every move is calculated and nothing is taken for granted. They cannot permit emotions to guide them—they must be alert and watch for dangers. But in Joseph's case, God's involvement caused the jailer to recognize that Joseph was no ordinary criminal. Joseph was trusted and given responsibility to the degree that "the chief jailer did not supervise anything under Joseph's charge because the Lord was with him" (v. 23). What an amazing turn of events!

A BLESSED LIFE IN PRISON

"Whatever he did, the Lord made to prosper" (v. 23). There is no other explanation for the astounding course of Joseph's life. Seldom are the two words *prison* and *blessing* used in the same sentence. Imprisonment is not usually considered a blessing. Yet, even in prison, Joseph was working under the mighty hand of God.

Talk about a miracle! No matter what Joseph did, God blessed it. His hands were blessed of the Lord, who was using him for positive ministry in the jail. When we are going through a tough time, we think we cannot possibly be living within the blessings of the Lord. But our God is able to make even the most horrible situation into a blessing.

- In prison, a missionary pastor from Managua, Nicaragua, led over 700 prisoners to Christ and baptized over 500 converts.

- In the midst of the Chinese Communist Revolution, Mao Tse-tung provided radios for much of the population and established Mandarin Chinese as the national language. God was preparing for the harvest of millions of Chinese souls through electronic evangelism.

- While imprisoned for Christ, the apostle Paul wrote to the Philippians regarding God's use of his imprisonment to spread the gospel: "Now I want you to know, brethren, that my circumstances have turned out for the greater progress of the gospel, so that my imprisonment in the cause of Christ has become well known throughout the whole praetorian guard and to everyone else, and that most of the brethren, trusting in the Lord because of my imprisonment, have far more courage to speak the word of God without fear" (Philippians 1:12-14).

It is a mistake for us to assume our location and circumstances determine how God blesses us. God often uses storms and difficult times to get our attention and reveal His power and glory to us. In the crucible of fire and stormy waters, the faith of the true believer is revealed. The apostle James said, "Blessed is the man who endures temptation; for when he has been approved, he will receive the crown of life which the Lord has promised to those who love Him" (James 1:12, NKJV).

God can and does use impossible situations to reveal His marvelous glory and prove that His plan will not be hindered by negative circumstances. When we feel hopeless, God is at His best! He proved that with Joseph. Though he was in prison, his life was flourishing. God was touching him, and he was being used of God to minister to others. It wasn't as he might have pictured it, but still the fruits of God's blessing were evident. To those who feel your lot in life means you cannot achieve anything productive—look at Joseph. Even in prison, he was doing good because the hand of the Lord was upon him. It is the same with each of us. When God's hand is upon us, the extraordinary occurs.

Samson was a young man who had many problems. He fell in love with the wrong kind of women. He frequented the wrong places and got into serious trouble. But when the Spirit of the Lord would come upon him, extraordinary things occurred.

Joseph was ready and God used that readiness. There is a process at work and the next big step was about to occur. He did not know it at the time and was not looking for an angle to exploit for his personal comfort. It is just the way God works. A simple day, nothing unusual, going about his daily chores, when there it is—an unexpected opportunity. God was setting everything in place. His life would never be the same after he became acquainted with the two employees of the Pharaoh.

Have you noticed that in your own life? The big moments with God are seldom planned. You don't get up one morning and expect the day to be life-changing. We are most often surprised by this kind of thing. I sense that Moses must have been surprised when, while tending his father-in-law's flock, a burning bush caught his attention. There was nothing extraordinary about the bush, except that it was burning and was not being consumed. Moses was intrigued and he approached, not knowing it was the beginning of the most incredible journey of his life.

Seldom do we get advance notice of God's plan. Instead, when we are faithful in serving Him and others, He does awesome things in us. That's what happened to Joseph as he waited on the prisoners. It was a normal day, as far as he could tell. Little did he know that his cellmates would offer him a life-changing opportunity.

Two rather unusual men who served in the king's palace were imprisoned because they had angered the king. On the day described, they had dreamed dreams which they could not understand. Joseph, the dreamer, was strategically and providentially placed in their paths. Isn't it amazing how God works? This was hardly mere coincidence.

God is omniscient and all-knowing. He knows everything about you and is never caught off guard by anything. What you need for today has been graciously provided.

They wished for their dreams to be interpreted. Joseph began to tell them the meaning of their dreams. He told the first that his dream was good. In three days, on Pharaoh's birthday, he would be reinstated and things would go back to what they had been. What a relief that must have been to the cupbearer. Joseph asks for a favor of the cupbearer: "Only keep me in mind when it goes well with you, and please do me a kindness by mentioning me to Pharaoh, and get me out of this house. For I was in fact kidnapped from the land of the Hebrews, and even here I have done nothing that they should have put me into the dungeon" (Genesis 40:14, 15).

His request was not inappropriate. Joseph knew the cupbearer would be in a position to assist him once he returned to the palace. Joseph was human enough to resent the fact that he was unjustly confined in prison. He simply needed a favor.

Next was the baker. After hearing about the good fortune of his buddy, the cupbearer, the baker was anxious to hear his fortune. Joseph operated with integrity here. He did not give the baker false hope. He looked him in the eye and said, "It's over—you will be hanged in three days!" As challenging as it was, Joseph again chose to do the right thing.

In three days, Joseph's words came to pass. We would like to think that the first thing the cupbearer did upon his restoration to the palace was tell the king about Joseph. But he didn't! He forgot him. The opening verse of chapter 41 says: "Now it happened at the end of two full years. . . ." Joseph stayed in jail for 24 extra months. How disappointing that must have been. Surely, he felt he would be remembered after all he had done to help others. But he was still stuck in prison.

So how do we handle things when those we depend on let us down? In those first few days after the cupbearer was released, I'm sure Joseph got his hopes up, but nothing happened. How do we cope in this situation?

Simple. You get up every morning like you did before and go about your life in the same way. You entrust everything to God and you wait for His timing. If God is in it, then it comes to pass in His time. If not, then you accept that God has a better plan for you than the one you anticipated.

Now, as you read this, you think, *That's easy for you—you are not here in this situation dealing with all these problems.* You're right, but God does understand your situation. He has never lost sight of where you are or what you are doing. From the beginning, we have come to understand that He has a plan and He is committed to work things out.

After reading this prison experience of Joseph, three principles linger in my mind.

1. *If we have the right attitude, God can make a prison a place of ministry and effectiveness.* When you think of a prison, you don't often think of effective ministry and fertile soil, unless you are a man like Chuck Colson. He rose from the ashes of public shame and humiliation during the Nixon years to build a ministry that reaches and disciples prisoners. His testimony and subsequent work among prison inmates are sparkling reminders that God can take life's dark lumps of coal and cause them to shine like diamonds.

2. *If you place your full confidence in man, you are sure to be disappointed.* Man is fallible. Too often, we place our trust in human flesh. We are disappointed when we do,. Only in God can we place our confidence. We can rely upon His righteousness. When my sister and I were praying for an urgent need in her family, I was driving to church service talking to God about the situation. The Spirit impressed me to call my sister and tell her these words: "When you get to the point you feel 'I am all I

have,' you will find I am all you need!" It was true then and it is still true today. Our source is the Lord. God would ultimately use the cupbearer, whom Joseph had helped, as a catalyst in getting Pharaoh to call for Joseph. But God was at work in Joseph's life all the time. The same is true for you and me—only God can do for our lives what needs to be done.

3. *God's timing and ways are past our understanding.* I marvel at God's timing. He doesn't move when I think He should, which sometimes frustrates me. There are times I want God to come on the scene and deliver me with might and power, but God says to wait. Part of the process of serving Him is understanding that we can't move God against His will or plan.

Listen to the comforting words of God spoken through His prophet Isaiah: "'For My thoughts are not your thoughts, neither are your ways My ways,' declares the Lord. 'For as the heavens are higher than the earth, so are My ways higher than your ways, and My thoughts than your thoughts'" (55:8, 9).

While we may not know God's timing, we are sure His timing is always right on schedule. Mary and Martha were sure the Lord was too late for their deceased brother. What they did not understand was that God had a better plan than they could imagine.

The same was true for Joseph. Waiting for God in an Egyptian prison was excruciatingly painful. But, we know God had a better plan. His plan was going to benefit not only Joseph, but also his father, brothers and their entire household. God sees the bigger picture. My human weakness is to be frustrated when God does not move in what I consider a timely fashion. Waiting is hard, but while God never moves on my clock, He is never late!

Now before the year of famine came, two sons were born to Joseph, whom Asenath, the daughter of Potiphera priest of On, bore to him. And Joseph named the first-born Manasseh, "For," he said, "God has made me forget all my trouble and all my father's household." And he named the second Ephraim, "For," he said, "God has made me fruitful in the land of my affliction."

Genesis 41:50-52

CHAPTER SIX

WHEN GOD MAKES ALL THINGS NEW

There is something about newness that is attractive. Why else would we trade a reliable car for a newer one? We will pay more money for the newer car, even though we have been quite comfortable in the older model. The fact of having the new car means we no longer have to deal with the problems of the old one. We somehow believe this new model will be better, freeing us from our frustration with the old.

We do that with a lot of things. We discard the old for the new, not because the old is no longer serviceable to us, but because we crave the feelings that come from having something new. It's fresh and offers tremendous hope for the coming days. We are tired of the old and want something new and exciting.

Some of us reach out to the new because the old makes us uncomfortable. The old things represent pain and sorrow that we would rather not have anymore, so we desire the day when the new comes and the old is forgotten.

The same is true for this part of Joseph's life. After he worked through all the bad stuff, it is exciting to read what God did to make all things right. Remember, Joseph had been through an incredible journey after he was betrayed by his brothers and sold. He spent time as a slave, was harassed and lied about, and sent to prison for several years. After 13 years, he was made second to Pharaoh and became a powerful ruler in Egypt. But how did he work through all the stuff left over from his devastating years?

- Did he forgive his brothers?

- How did he work through his anger and disappointment at Potiphar's wife?

- Who counseled him through his resentment at being placed in prison for something he did not do?

- What did he say to the cupbearer the next time they met in Pharaoh's palace?

Some incredible things occurred. After Joseph interpreted Pharaoh's dream, he was appointed to a key position that required wisdom for preserving the nation during a famine. Although Joseph was successful, there was unfinished business in his life. His family was far away, and as far as his father was concerned, Joseph was dead.

His brothers had moved on with their lives. Although there were unpleasant memories regarding what they had done, for the most part, Joseph was not one of them anymore.

Before we get too spiritual with what God was doing, let's remember that pain hurts! Some people boast that they never get hurt by words and people don't affect them—that's simply not true. Everyone has a sore spot and the Enemy will find it and poke it from time to time, and it does hurt. We are left to wonder:

- Did Joseph miss his family?
- Did he ever wonder what happened to his younger brother and his dad?
- Did he ever feel residual disappointment in his older brothers?

He must have! Every remembrance was probably painful. Every mental image of that pit, the journey and the betrayal of his brothers offered Joseph an opportunity to become bitter. But he resisted. This is an incredible thing to consider.

Such a lack of bitterness and anger is the result of a sovereign move of God. No man can do that, and no therapist can arrange that; God has to do it. If God can make a world from nothing, He can change the way we look at people, circumstances and painful memories. Does such an act of God remove our ability to remember what happened? I don't think so. Rather, I believe this divine action of God penetrates the heart and allows us to remember, without pain, the things that have bothered us from the past. When God is finished with this process, we are able to look at the person who wronged us and not hurt anymore. We still remember, and the scar is always present as a reminder, but discomfort is no longer there. New skin has grown to cover the affected area.

There is a small scar on the inside of my right hand. It is a circular scar from my attempt to throw a broken soft drink bottle. The glass tore my skin and caused a deep wound. I wore a bandage for some time and, being right-handed, I suffered much because of it. Eventually, it healed, and today there is neither pain nor tenderness. The healing was complete. The scar reminds me of what happened, but I cannot feel the pain anymore. It is the same with God's marvelous healing power in the heart of the offended. I testify to you that it is possible.

Quite a few years ago, I preached a message one Sunday evening from Matthew 5 and 6 on forgiveness. I stressed the point that when we are the offender, we must make the first move to ask forgiveness from those we offended. Yet, I believe the passage also teaches that if I am offended, I must forgive even before I am asked. I know some will disagree, but I believe forgiveness is not something you withhold. If I withhold forgiveness to those who wronged me, I may never find release in my heart.

Such was the nature of my message on this evening to our church family. There was a sovereign move of God and quite a few came to the altar to talk with God about forgiveness. At the end of the service, a woman asked for time to share with the congregation what had occurred in her heart. It was obvious there was deep emotion in what she was feeling, and the following is a summation of her remarks that night:

> When you were preaching tonight, I was struck by the memory of my childhood. I have never revealed to anyone, including my husband, that when I was a child, my father did something really bad to me. Over the years, the emotional hurt that accumulated was more than I could stand. I wanted and felt I needed my father to tell me he was sorry. He never did. I became an adult and married. My children were his grandchildren, and although I felt distant from my father, our relationship continued. I waited for him to deal with this continuing, unresolved feeling that was beginning to be a wall in my heart, guarding against everything. I loved the Lord with all my heart and tried to serve Him faithfully. To the observer, I appeared to have it all together. On the inside, I was crushed. Every time I prayed, I could not find release. I was waiting for him to apologize, believing his apology would set me free. He never did. At his funeral, I waited until no one was looking. Standing over his casket, I whispered, "I hate you. You never told me you were sorry!" I kept our secret all these years, but tonight I felt God speaking to me as the message was preached. The Lord said, "He's never going to tell you he was sorry. But you can be free. I will heal you." When I came forward, I felt God's Spirit in a different way. There was a release, and I know it's over now!

Her testimony moved me, and I watched her to see the evidence. The change was clear. The bitter spirit she had been noted for was gone. There was joy in her life. It was remarkable! Does she still remember what her father did? Of course. Indelibly etched into her brain are the bad memories, but by God's grace, the hurting is over. The bitterness that had ensnared her spirit was broken like a twig when she released her situation to the Lord. I tell you, only God can do that!

For some of us, the bitter memories of yesterday keep us from reaching our full potential. There are those moments we wish we could forget, but they are forever with us, or so we think. God's message to your weary soul is that yesterday is over.

When God called Moses from a burning bush in the Sinai desert as he kept his father-in-law's flock, it was a turning point in his life. Ultimately, his life was never the same because of what happened at that bush. As I read it again, I am struck by something that few of us remember. We vividly remember that God told Moses that He was aware of the plight of His people in Egypt, and that Moses had been chosen to be their deliverer. You may recall that Moses was the reluctant leader, citing his many shortcomings:

- "Who am I to go to Pharaoh?" (Exodus 3:11).
- "The elders of Israel will not receive me" (v. 13).
- "They won't believe You sent me" (4:1).
- "I am not a good speaker" (v. 10).
- "Why not someone else?" (v. 13).

Finally, God convinced Moses to go. The last thing God said to Moses as he prepared to leave for Egypt was, in my opinion, the most profound. In Exodus 4:19 we read, "Now the Lord said to Moses in Midian, 'Go back to Egypt, for all the men who were seeking your life are dead.'" Maybe that was the reason Moses was so reluctant—he was afraid of yesterday. Remember, the reason he was in that desert was because of an unfortunate mistake on his part, 40 years earlier. He had tried to take matters into his own hands and deliver Israel—one dead Egyptian at a time! Going back to Egypt meant facing what he had left undone there. He did not want to do that! God knew this too! Gently He whispered into Moses' spirit, "Yesterday is over. Forget it and move on."

Those can be words of release for some people today. Your mistakes and failures have been thrown in your face by the Enemy every time you tried to serve God. *What if people find out?* Satan whispers to our minds. Well, I ask you, what embarrassment will you have if you try to move on? Friend, the devil is a liar! If God has forgiven you and you have placed it under the blood of Jesus—it's over! God never deals with us according to our past—He is only concerned with our future. You can cast off the shackles of yesterday and accept Christ's invitation to step into a new day, where yesterday is over and tomorrow is brighter than it's ever been, because Jesus is Lord of it all!

There is something else about yesterday you need to forget: your accomplishments and achievements. Like failures, they can weigh you down if you linger too long, admiring and appreciating what they represent. You may become fixated on what you did and fail to realize it was God at work in your achievement. Both extremes can be deadly. Every day is a new day.

A powerful principle was taught in the manna God sent the children of Israel. The instructions were simply to gather each morning what they would need for that day. God told Moses to warn the people about hoarding the manna. In fact, God told Moses that if the people tried to gather two days' bread at a time, during the night the second day's bread would rot. God wanted them to trust Him every day just like He wants us to trust Him. We cannot linger in the past or move ahead of God; we must walk daily, in the provisions of His grace.

How do we know Joseph was recreated in his spirit regarding his hurts and disappointments? When Joseph's wife gave birth to their first son, his name was *Manasseh*, meaning "God has made me forget all my trouble and all my father's household" (Genesis 41:51). I seldom read that without tears, because as I read about this man's trials and afflictions, I want to say: "How can this be?" He was a prime candidate for failure and discouragement, but he held to God's promise and saw the Lord do what seemed impossible. He survived without losing his mind. The long nightmare that began on the cart headed toward Egypt had now ended. No longer was there pain when he recalled the past days. Rather, he rejoiced in a God who was able to take all that life had done to him and replace it with joy. Joseph knew something you and I know—God's grace and strength will get us through anything. As the days come, God creates something new from the painful experiences. He replaces pain with joy. That's God's sustaining grace.

In Biblical times, children were often named to remember significant times. Every time Joseph called his son's name, he smiled. The mere mention of Manasseh reminded Joseph of an incredible God who took what men meant for evil and made it good. The hurt of the past was over and God had made everything new.

TOMORROW

Finish each day and be done with it.

You have done what you could;

Some blunders and absurdities no doubt crept in;

forget them as soon as you can.

Tomorrow is a new day;

you shall begin it serenely and with too high a spirit

to be encumbered with your old nonsense.

–Ralph Waldo Emerson

*A*nd the seven years of famine began to come, just as Joseph had said, then there was famine in all the lands; but in all the land of Egypt there was bread. So when all the land of Egypt was famished, the people cried out to Pharaoh for bread; and Pharaoh said to all the Egyptians, "Go to Joseph; whatever he says to you, you shall do." When the famine was spread over all the face of the earth, then Joseph opened all the storehouses, and sold to the Egyptians; and the famine was severe in the land of Egypt. And the people of all the earth came to Egypt to buy grain from Joseph, because the famine was severe in all the earth. Now Jacob saw that there was grain in Egypt, and Jacob said to his sons, "Why are you staring at one another?" And he said, "Behold, I have heard that there is grain in Egypt; go down there and buy some for us from that place, so that we may live and not die." Then ten brothers of Joseph went down to buy grain from Egypt.

Genesis 41:54-57; 42:1-3

CHAPTER SEVEN

WHEN THINGS HAPPEN YOU DON'T UNDERSTAND

D o you ever just shake your head in amazement when you read the Bible? There are so many incredible twists in the Bible, things inconceivable, except to God. One reason we are so amazed by these events is because we are limited by our capacity to think and see only the present and the memories of our past. We have no way of knowing what the future holds, but God does. He is eternal and He not only sees all, He is present in all. Your future is not future to Him. He inhabits all of time and space and everything is present to Him.

As God looks at your life, He does not see merely a single incident or event—He views it in the context of the total picture. Therefore, God is not dismayed by a single act or event, because He knows your future. He ordains and works in your life as a total package. It is the reason some of the things that happen to us are so extraordinary. What may appear to be a total tragedy is not, because God has arranged something so glorious that the present tragedy, when viewed in light of the total picture, can look rather insignificant.

This principle is clear when I look at the circumstances of Joseph's life. No one could have predicted the outcome based on what was happening. It appeared Joseph had taken a wrong turn on the road of life and the fates deemed him lost—but not God. He has a marvelous way of turning things around.

We like comfort, and in most cases, it is fine with us if nothing changes. Our lives are stable. Though some things may not be to our liking, we accept them as predictable. That's what we like about the status quo—it's predictable! We get up each day, knowing just how everything will be, and as long as nothing changes, we can manage. Nothing unsettles us like an unexpected phone call or letter. Everything is predictable and logically organized until the doctor's office calls to report there are problems with the X-rays or tests.

Thinking theologically is a tough thing to do. It works against our human and horizontal perspective on life. Thinking vertically is a discipline few have mastered. We much prefer to live in the here-and-now realm, seeing life as others see it, dealing with the realities we can touch, analyze, prove and explain. We are much more comfortable with the tactile, the familiar, the logic shaped by our culture and lived out in our times. But God offers a better way to live, one that requires faith as it lifts us above the drag and grind of our immediate little world, opens new dimensions of thought and introduces a perspective without human limitations. In order to enter this better way, we must train ourselves to think theologically. Once we've made the switch our focus turns away from ourselves, removing us from the self-centered realm of existence and opening the door of our minds to a God-centered frame of reference, where all things begin and end with Him.[1]

What we really want is peace and contentment. Further frustrating our world is the knowledge that sometimes, it is God at work, unsettling the arrangements for us to consider His ways and plans. He has a way of doing that.

Joseph had been through more than 20 years of the unpredictable since his brothers sold him. He was in a place of power and prominence—his life was good. But God was not through with him yet. Bringing Joseph's dreams to reality was only one part of the puzzle—it was not the ultimate plan. God had other pots simmering on the burner for Joseph and his family.

The famine in Egypt may have been God's plan for bringing Joseph to his position as lord over Pharaoh's government, but the famine had bigger implications for a Jewish family, living in Canaan. Jacob and his sons were wondering how they were going to feed the family. Word reached them that grain was available in Egypt, so his sons hitched the mules to the wagons and made the journey. Their lives would never be the same. God was working all the components of a master plan that would ultimately save Jacob and his whole family. Deliverance and salvation was coming despite the deeds of evil brothers, the depression of a lamenting father and the skillful planning of a young dreamer. God was in control and it was His plan guiding this drama.

Like you and me, Joseph was forced to deal with circumstances as they came, believing God would work His plan. To do so, there were living principles that guided his path. They worked for Joseph and they can work for you as well. Consider each of them carefully and see how they apply to your personal walk with God when things don't go according to your plans.

1. *Remember who God is.* It sounds too simple, but this is the starting place in coming to grips with moments that shake our world—moments when you want to throw your hands in the air and declare that you cannot go on. After all, you can only take so much! We have all been there too many times.

We are forced to admit that the God of Jacob and Joseph saw what they could not see and He knew what they did not know and He understood what they could not understand. His ways are past our understanding. We don't have all the information or the knowledge to manage the affairs of the world. Sometimes, Kathy and I realize that managing our little house of four is more than we can do—much less the more than 6 billion people on the face of the earth. But every minute of every day, God watches everything and never panics. Amazing!

One thing is clear as you read the Bible—when God works, He does so perfectly! Job was a man of great prosperity and wealth, which was unfortunately all wiped out in one day. Forsaken by his friends and family, Job counted

God as his faithful friend. He knew that what God does in a human life is always done perfectly. So from the ash heap of his broken life, the narrative of Job reveals:

> Then Job arose and tore his robe and shaved his head, and he fell to the ground and worshiped. And he said, "Naked I came from my mother's womb, and naked I shall return there. The Lord gave and the Lord has taken away. Blessed be the name of the Lord" (Job 1:20, 21).

2. *Things are not always as they appear.* Take another look at Joseph. Sold by his brothers into slavery, his life appeared to be tragic. In God's eyes, it was part of a process that brought Joseph to a greater moment of God's revealed power and glory. Did God want Joseph to suffer? No! But in the bigger picture, God was incorporating what Joseph's brothers meant for harm into His plan for the salvation of Jacob's entire family.

In my first pastorate, a wonderful elderly lady approached me one Sunday morning. Her youngest son, Howard, was in the hospital and needed prayer. She squeezed my hand and asked if I could visit him. I made my way to Baptist Hospital in Winston-Salem the next morning and found her son. Howard Breeden had been an alcoholic most of his life and had spent numerous nights in the county jail. What I saw on that morning was a dying man. His body was bloated, his color was very yellow. Because he was on a breathing machine, it was almost impossible for him to talk. However, we managed to communicate. When I inquired about his soul, he negatively shook his head.

"Do you know that Jesus died for your sins?" I asked. "Although you have not served the Lord, He is ready to forgive you if you are truly sorry and want to accept Him. Can you understand that?" He nodded affirmatively.

"Do you want to accept Jesus Christ as your Savior?" Again he nodded. Taking his hand, I prayed with this dying man. I don't pretend to understand all the theology of how God saves a sinner like Howard Breeden, but I do know when the Holy Spirit comes into a room. What a powerful presence of God filled that hospital room! Tears filled the hollow sockets of his eyes and he cried out to God, "Save me!" I know God did.

Howard died a few hours after that prayer. I went to Sister Breeden's home and shared with her what had happened during my visit. She wept tears of joy and asked if we could have the funeral at our church. I assured her we could. As I left the house, I sensed God at work. Howard's alcoholic brothers and sisters came, totally oblivious to the transforming power of God. We gathered our church family and filled the choir and sanctuary for the funeral of a known alcoholic. God touched us all.

Leaving the grave site, I asked the oldest sister to arrange for the family to all be in church on Sunday morning to support their mother. She agreed. They filled several rows of the sanctuary. God moved powerfully that morning, saving 18 members of the family. One of the brothers did not attend because he was at home drunk. He came the following week under heavy conviction, and I was privileged to pray the sinner's prayer with him. Before I moved from that pastorate, I took 41 members into the church as a direct result of Howard Breeden's death.

I don't understand it, but I tell you, God can take your tragedies and turn them to victories. Just as He did for Joseph, He will do for you. When you think things are at their worst, God can work in an incredible way. It will boggle your mind and amaze everyone.

This same principle applies to Joseph's father. Remember, Jacob thought Joseph was dead. Jacob lamented to his sons in Genesis 42:36, "All these things are against me." We now know that was not true, but Jacob didn't. God was at work on Jacob's behalf. All he could see was his loss. That's only natural. The point to remember is that God is never surprised by our circumstances.

Faith does not walk by sight—faith walks by a belief in God and His amazing ability to work in our lives, regardless of the negative circumstances.

3. *God's grace is sufficient.* I don't know any other way to say it, but sometimes life stinks! Sometimes we are left with brokenness and emptiness in our lives. We cry out to God for strength and wonder why certain things happen. It is the mystery of God's ways that often leaves us wanting to know *why* things occur. Some tragedies are never understood, while others seem logical, although they hurt just as deeply.

A drunken driver is killed by his own decision. It is so tragic, especially if he or she is a member of your family. Can we find some understanding? When a young mother and her two children are killed by that same person, we shake our heads and wonder why.

Some things will never be explained. Nowhere in Scripture are we ever promised understanding. We used to sing the old hymn, "We'll Understand It Better By and By." I am not so sure about that. Does God owe me an explanation? Why should God have to give any answers? Some things happen, and we are left to pick up the pieces and accept God's sovereignty. It almost never makes sense. In moments like these we see the provision of sustaining grace and its sufficiency for our lives. While I don't understand everything, I can manage to move on with my life because of God's marvelous grace.

If we are guided by our own feelings, despair is always going to be our response. Our feelings are too transient and unsettled. We must lean hard on the faithfulness of God in times of uncertainty, knowing He cares for us so intimately, He will make sure we survive.

From my personal experiences, I can tell you that you can depend on God to get you through. As I grow older, I become more convinced of God's commitment to get me through the tough moments in my life. He will not abandon me on the side of life's highway. He is beside me, within me and around me to provide strength beyond my own. I have a constant hope in His ability to work out the difficult matters of my life. I may not see the way, nor understand the process, but I can be certain that God is faithful to me.

One of my favorite verses of Scripture is in Hebrews 13:5, 6. Once, while riding out an emotional storm that rocked my boat, I read this verse in my morning devotions and its message stuck. Listen to the writer's words: "For He Himself has said, 'I will never leave you nor forsake you.' So we may boldly say: 'The Lord is my helper; I will not fear. What can man do to me?' " (*NKJV*).

He is never going to leave you . . .

- When your mother dies
- When your spouse leaves you unexpectedly and without cause
- When the doctors cannot give a good prognosis
- When your children forsake you
- When you come to the end of your life.

You can count on the continual presence of God for every moment and every situation of your life. Talk about insurance! God, the Creator of all that is, determined you will never face anything alone! No wonder the writer of Hebrews concludes with "What can man do to me?"

4. *God has everything under control.* After reading the entire account of Joseph's life, the famine makes sense to me. God used the tragedy of this dearth to bring Jacob to Egypt. Egypt was where God's provision was established. It is unlikely that Jacob or his sons would have ever traveled to Egypt, had it not been for the famine. So God dried up the land and forced His reluctant servants to seek His provision. Maybe He closed down the plant where I worked to force me to look for the job He really wanted for me.

Like my own life, Joseph and Jacob knew nothing of the future. They had to live each day by faith. From time to time, I must remind myself God controls every king, every president, every decision and every action. Nothing slips by Him. He works His plan regardless of men and angels. I leave these reminders to you who have struggled to understand the unusual ways of God.

He keeps everything going in the right direction. This is one of life's most amazing concepts. God never misses a beat. Listen to Jesus: "Are not two sparrows sold for a cent? And yet not one of them will fall to the ground apart from your Father. But the very hairs of your head are all numbered. Therefore do not fear; you are of more value than many sparrows" (Matthew 10:29-31).

He won't allow circumstances to overwhelm me. From Paul's writings we are encouraged that God knows our limits; He will not allow the Enemy to inflict more on us than we are able to manage. "No temptation has overtaken you but such as is common to man; and God is faithful, who will not allow you to be tempted beyond what you are able, but with the temptation will provide the way of escape also, that you may be able to endure it" (1 Corinthians 10:13).

He brings everything together in accordance with His plan and His will. When I watch the news and hear of major developments determined by world leaders, I smile. As a believer, I am convinced it all works in accordance with God's plan and His will. The president of the United States may be the announced leader of the free world, but he is really not in charge. The leaders of the United Nations may determine the course of action that will impact millions, but none of them are in charge. That billing goes to the Most High God. It is He who puts men in their place and determines the course of life in this world. Not one decision or action is made without God's knowledge. When the last chapter is written in your life and mine, it will be God who turns the pages. I rest in His amazing peace, knowing He is in complete control of all that touches my life.

Now Joseph was the ruler over the land; he was the one who sold to all the people of the land. And Joseph's brothers came and bowed down to him with their faces to the ground.
Genesis 42:6

CHAPTER EIGHT

WHEN GOD DOES WHAT HE PROMISES

Not long ago, I watched a show where people were asked whom they trusted to keep their promises. Parents were high on the list, as were spouses. But as you might expect, politicians were very low. When they were asked to name the last person in the world they would trust to keep their promises, almost everyone said, "Politicians!" It seems as though we have come to expect dishonesty from those we elect to represent us in the government.

One of the great chapters of the story of Joseph revolves around his consistent belief that his brothers would one day come to bow down before him. Joseph's life from age 17 until 30 did not look like a dream—it resembled a nightmare! There was nothing happening in his life to give a remote idea of grandeur or destiny. Tragedy, deception, unfair treatment and abandonment were his constant companions. There must have been days when Joseph wondered if his dreams would ever come true. Steadfastly, Joseph moved ahead, believing and trusting God to complete what was birthed in his heart years before.

We know now that approximately 13 years passed before Joseph settled into his new job. He married and had two sons. He was the second most powerful man, next to Pharaoh. The seven years of plenty came and were followed by seven years of famine, just as Joseph predicted. Fortunately, Pharaoh listened to Joseph's counsel and allowed him to store enough surplus grain to keep Egypt alive during the severe famine. However, this famine was not only in Egypt—Canaan was also affected. Jacob and his family depleted their supplies and needed food. When he heard of the grain available in Egypt, he sent his sons (except Benjamin) to buy grain. What none of them knew, including Joseph, was that God was planning a family reunion. When Joseph's brothers arrived in Egypt, they found themselves facedown, on the ground, in front of a man they did not yet recognize—their brother Joseph!

Remember Joseph's dreams at the age of 17: "Please listen to this dream which I have had; for behold, we were binding sheaves in the field, and lo, my sheaf rose up and also stood erect; and behold, your sheaves gathered around and bowed down to my sheaf" (Genesis 37:6, 7). Just as Joseph told them, they were now bowing to honor a man who reigned over them. It would be funny, if it were not so serious.

The beauty of this episode in Joseph's life reveals the powerful principle that what God promises, He always brings to pass! Thirteen years before, it was only a dream in the heart of a young teenage boy. But God did it and the reality was before him—his brothers were doing just what he told them God said they would do.

As I consider how unlikely it was for such a thing to happen, three things about this young man come to mind:

- Joseph had no marketable skills, because he was not trained in any vocation. He did not work with his hands as his brothers did. Subsequently, his ability to generate wealth and gain power and authority would not likely happen. As far as they were concerned, he was the least likely to succeed. But obviously, God saw things differently.

- Joseph was younger than most of Jacob's children. All of the 10 brothers were born before him. He would not command great respect in the family under normal circumstances because of his age, notwithstanding his volatile relationship with his brothers.

- While Jacob was a friendly man and one with considerable assets in Canaan, he had no connections with Egyptian royalty. Therefore, no one in power was pulling for Joseph. His ancestry was not impressive to Pharaoh and he was not involved in work that connected him with the hierarchy of Egyptian politics. Have you ever noticed how God searches out those no one else would suspect?

Remember how David was anointed to be king? The one no one considered was the one God chose. Why? God told Samuel the answer: "Man looks at the outward appearance, but the Lord looks at the heart" (1 Samuel 16:7).

God raised Joseph to a place of unparalleled power. He stood as Egypt's brightest star because God is not swayed by what others think or do. His plans are sovereign and man cannot stop what God ordains. Yet, He will not work where He is not given full control. When it appears there might be a way someone would think man orchestrated the miracle, God will alter the situation.

Another story from Scripture illustrates this principle. Gideon was called of God to fight the Midianites. So he gathered an army of approximately 32,000 soldiers. As they prepared for battle, God said to Gideon, "The people who are with you are too many for Me to give Midian into their hands, lest Israel become boastful, saying, 'My own power has delivered me'" (Judges 7:2).

Why was that important? God would not allow Israel to boast in her own strength. He wanted Israel to trust Him. With 32,000 soldiers, there would be the report of Gideon's great army defeating the enemies. The result would have been that the people placed their trust in Gideon and his army. However, Gideon was not the resource of Israel—God was! You and I must not forget that our feeble attempts are insufficient. All our energies and efforts will fall short. Only when we trust completely in God will we be successful.

Do you find certain passages in Scripture amusing? Here's one that might make you smile. God instructed Gideon to tell the soldiers who wanted to go home to just go ahead and leave. Gideon must have been amazed when 22,000 picked up their suitcases and went home! So much for his brave soldiers. God then told Gideon that he still had too many. So a water-lapping contest whittled the group to 300. God was pleased; though the victory was already assured, He wanted the people to learn to trust Him.

With only 300 soldiers against the massive Midianite army, no one would believe that the size or might of Gideon's army was the key. It was God who brought the victories in their lives, just as it is with you and me. God will not share His glory with any person or nation. He is God alone. In the moments when you determine you have no one to help you, you will find God at His best.

So as we observe what happened to Joseph, we can see it could only have been the hand of God that brought Joseph from the prison to the palace. No one could take the credit, and the only one to be commended was God himself. Years earlier, God had spoken a plan into the heart of this young man that required faith beyond Joseph's own ability to believe. His unwavering faith in God's promises ultimately brought him to the realization of those early dreams.

1. *His brothers could not stop the fulfillment of his dreams.* Their hatred and jealousy motivated them to a despicable act of betrayal. They thought they were finished with Joseph, but didn't take into account that God never forgets His

promises. God never forgets His people, and He never forgets those who deal wickedly with us.

2. *Potiphar's wife could not stop the fulfillment of his dreams.* Working through her fleshly desires, she attempted to bring Joseph into her world of deception and deviance. Her power and prominence were an ominous threat to a young man far from home. But Joseph stayed true to his commitment.

3. *His cellmates could not stop the fulfillment of his dreams.* Those who were in positions to help him, forgot him. Their omission would have meant despair if Joseph had looked for a man to bring about God's promises. Joseph did not need a servant of Pharaoh, an ally in the government or a rich uncle. His God was in charge of his life and, no matter whom or what he faced, he knew God would fulfill His word.

If God has spoken to your heart in the past, I encourage you to start making preparations for the fulfillment of His word—God will not fail you! The final chapters of your life have not been written yet. It is never too late—He *will* do what He said!

You can count on the scoffers and mockers, especially if you make your promises public. They are always there to tell you . . .

- it cannot possibly happen.

- God was not really talking to you.

- God does not work like that anymore.

But don't be discouraged. The answer is coming. The hardest part is the waiting. We can do a lot of things, but waiting is excruciatingly difficult. The Bible contains many accounts of mistakes made by impatient people.

- Abraham and Sarah could not wait for God to provide them with a son, so they enlisted Hagar's participation and the world is still feeling the effects of the ensuing family discord.

- Moses knew he was destined to be a deliverer, but his impatience caused him to run ahead of God. The result was a dead Egyptian and Moses' flight to the desert, where he spent 40 years shackled by past mistakes.

- King Saul was told to wait for the prophet Samuel to come to Gilgal and offer sacrifices. He grew impatient and offered the sacrifices himself—God rejected him as king.

In these and many other cases, human beings have struggled with the waiting part of God's promises. Often, they suffered the consequences of their impatience and in some cases they failed to inherit the promises previously given to them by God.

There were obviously times in Joseph's life when he wondered if God was going to do what He said. After he was betrayed, disappointed and frustrated, he must have been tempted to give up on his dreams. But he did not. Despite his trials, he maintained his confidence in God's ability to do what He promised.

To some of you, the outcome of what you have dreamed seems so impossible. Don't be discouraged. If God spoke those dreams into your life, He will bring them to fruition. It is the Enemy who causes you to doubt. Stand on the promises of God and wait for *His* timing.

Standing in a mud hole, making bricks for a wicked Pharaoh, the children of Israel cried out for deliverance from their slavery. Day after day, year after year, nothing seemed to happen. Generations slipped by and the people were still enslaved. The rational mind would say, "God has forgotten about His people." However, God had promised Abraham that his descendants would be slaves in a foreign land for 400 years and then deliverance would come. Though doubters lost hope in God's promises, God did not move from His word. A baby boy was born whose purpose was already ordained by God. He would be used of God to bring the children of Israel out of Egypt. However, even he would have to learn to wait on God. Eventually the time came when God said to Moses, "It's time."

Through a series of miracles, God's people moved to the land promised to their forefathers. As the Book of Joshua closes, the writer reminds us of God's faithfulness:

> So the Lord gave Israel all the land which He had sworn to give to their fathers, and they possessed it and lived in it. And the Lord gave them rest on every side, according to all that He had sworn to their fathers, and no one of all their enemies stood before them; the Lord gave all their enemies into their hand. Not one of the good promises which the Lord had made to the house of Israel failed; all came to pass (Joshua 21:43-45).

Did you catch that? Not one of God's promises failed to come to pass. Go back and read those final four words:

"All came to pass." Some of you need to grasp that truth in your spirit. Everything God has spoken, He will do. The skeptics wonder how this can be. It's simple—what God promises, He always brings to pass.

As a boy, I traveled with my father to a revival meeting he was conducting in the neighboring community of Bryson City, North Carolina. An elderly man came to the altar at the invitation. He was gloriously saved and testified of his conversion to the congregation. After he finished, his wife stood and told the church how God had promised to save her husband before he died. According to her testimony, 41 years before that night, God spoke to her heart and gave her this promise. After holding to that promise for so long, she saw the reality of what God had promised.

Young Joseph stood by his brothers and told them how they would have a divine destiny and they hated him for it. His father scolded him and encouraged him to hold his peace. Perhaps Joseph would have been better served to keep his silence, but the fact remains—God did what He promised.

GOD'S TIMETABLE

God works on His own timetable. God never gets in a hurry regarding His plans and promises concerning you. As we begin to see God for who He is, we understand that, as God is eternal and inhabits all time, He is not relegated to one perspective or period of your life. Rather, He views you in the total scope of your past, your present and your future. Sometimes we become impatient because we want God to move now. But God is not angry, nor is He anxious. He continues to work His mighty works and the end results will be fantastic.

Joseph moved from one event to the next, and God was not anxious or frustrated. Why? Because He sees the total plan clearly. We get in a hurry and often make mistakes because we do not always think every detail through. God does not make such mistakes because He is never in a hurry with our lives or His promises.

GOD FULFILLS HIS WORD

The story is told of a country preacher full of emotion, shouting his message in a small church. In his excitement speaking about the faithfulness of God, he shouted, "You can count on God! He will come through 99 times out of 100!" He missed it by one. Regardless of what is happening, what others are saying or how you feel, you can count on the faithfulness of God 100 times out of 100! Never once has God failed to meet one promise He made to His children or even to His enemies. Trace the promises of God throughout the Book and I challenge you to find one—just one—example of God failing to keep His promise. Don't waste your time—it's not there. God is perfect in all His ways and His faithfulness continues from generation to generation.

GOD'S PERFECT PLANS

Why does God promise us certain things, knowing they will not come to pass for an extended period of time? For one thing, promises are an anchor of hope for the soul. As we hold tightly to the promises of God, we look with anticipation and hope toward the future, knowing God will keep His word. Somewhere, perhaps reading this book, there is a mother who has held to the promises that God will save her prodigal children. The Enemy says, "God forgot." But she knows God will keep His word. So with hope, each day she reminds God of His promises, not because she thinks He has to be reminded, but to reinforce the hope in her soul.

For the person who is stuck in a dead-end career, keep holding to God's reassuring promise of fulfillment. Don't despair. The final chapters of your life are the exclusive property of God Almighty. He knows each step you take. You may feel you are wasting your time, but God is preparing you for a higher calling. In faithful obedience, follow Joseph's example, stay faithful and watch for God's hand to move you in the right direction.

As a father, I am overjoyed when I learn something about my boys they don't yet know. Maybe it's a gift or an announcement, but I know the details and they don't. Sometimes it is more than I can stand to smile and anticipate how pleased and happy they are going to be when the news is shared or the gift is unwrapped. In the same way, our Father sees our future and knows what is about to happen. He must smile with joy knowing how excited we are going to be when the day of fulfillment arrives. Just think . . . the day you have been holding to for so long will finally come.

*A*nd their father Israel said to them, "If it must be so, then do this: take some of the best products of the land in your bags, and carry down to the man as a present, a little balm and a little honey, aromatic gum and myrrh, pistachio nuts and almonds and take double the money in your hand, and take back in your hand the money that was returned in the mouth of your sacks; perhaps it was a mistake. Take your brother also, and arise, return to the man. And may God Almighty grant compassion in the sight of you the man, that he may release to you your other brother and Benjamin. And as for me, if I am bereaved of my children, I am bereaved."

Genesis 43:11-14

CHAPTER NINE

WHEN YOU DETERMINE TO DO THINGS GOD'S WAY

The hard thing about serving God is giving up control of our lives. We want to know what is going to happen and what we can expect. But God says, "Trust Me." Trusting is the hard part. We've heard the story of the man who fell from a cliff and fortunately grasped a protruding limb. Hanging for dear life, he called for help and heard a voice softly saying, "Turn loose and I will catch you." He responded, "Who are you?" "I am God, you can trust Me, turn loose and let Me catch you!" After a pause, the man began to call again, "Anyone else up there who can help?" It's the turning-loose part that is so hard for us.

Surrender is both the essence and one of the greatest difficulties of the Christian life. In many ways, it defines the Christian life. . . . Few of us enjoy being told what we can or can't do, whether it's by a spouse, a parent, a bureaucrat, or a boss. Surrender is thus an unnatural (or better, "supernatural") response to everyday life. Why? To be human is to desire control. A controlling person can't even imagine that he might be wrong or that someone else's perspective might make more sense or take into account something he hadn't thought of. In spiritual language, control is the absence of humility: "I know what is best, so it has to be done my way."[1]

There are two main characters in this story of Joseph. Early on we learn of the special bond between Joseph and Jacob, his father. We are actually told why Joseph was so loved—"Because he was the son of his old age" (37:3). Both are classic studies in our challenge to trust God with the issues and details of our lives. One is a man who has maneuvered and manipulated his way through life to gain everything he now holds dear. The other is the son who holds tightly to the dream he believes God has given him.

Be careful not to judge Jacob too harshly. Who wouldn't be apprehensive at this point in his life? As far as he is concerned, he has already lost Rachel and Joseph. Now his sons are talking about taking Benjamin to Egypt to satisfy some leader who is demanding his presence in exchange for food. It is more than he can take. Thus he laments, "All these things are against me" (42:36). One can only take so much sorrow in life, regardless of what you do. The load is bearing down on Jacob and the despair of his own soul cries, "If I be bereaved of my children, I am bereaved" (43:14, KJV).

When things go bad, and they do for all of us, we have a tendency to despair easily. We focus too closely on our potential insecurity and fail to trust God for what He knows is best. Although it is mentioned often, I have to keep reminding myself that Jacob could not see what God was doing. He was living this drama on a daily basis. The same is true of us. Each day brings new challenges that God wants us to process in light of His faithfulness to our lives and our knowledge of His divine care.

When I get weighed down with cares, God has to get my attention and remind me of His care for me. While driving to an appointment, I felt the Enemy begin to attack my faith and cause me to worry about the future. This has always been a point of vulnerability for me, and I have to keep up my guard against my tendency to panic about things. Driving down the road, I sensed the Enemy whispering in my ear all the dreadful things that could occur to me, my wife and our boys. For a brief moment, I began to feel a sense of dread and fear. I asked the Lord for divine strength and He began to fill my mind with memories of my grandmother, who trusted God for more than six decades. I thought of my grandfather, a pioneer preacher who lived to age 87 and died peacefully in the arms of God. I remember their stories of trials and tests during their ministry and their church-planting days and how God sustained them through apparent danger. I remembered my father and mother, who have served God faithfully and ministered to thousands through the years. Although they encountered trouble and distress, they were always kept by the power of God.

I recalled how God had preserved and kept Kathy and me through early years of need and how our family was so blessed. The presence of God began to fill my heart as I remembered how faithful God really is!

You, too, have a testimony of God's daily and continued faithfulness. Circumstances can be very negative in the present and we can feel an awesome load of stress and strain from life, but we must not panic or despair. God is our strength and shield. We can lean on Him and know He has never forsaken His own.

As for Joseph, his challenge was one that called for faith to rise above the visible circumstances. His life was marked by a series of unexplainable situations. Every time Joseph appeared to make progress, another negative circumstance changed the scenery and brought another challenge. For example, once he reached Potiphar's house and began to settle into his place as a servant, he became the focus of his master's attention. Potiphar could tell Joseph was not an ordinary slave—he was special.

We know from Scripture that God's hand was upon Joseph and everything he touched was blessed. In addition, everything in Potiphar's house was blessed because of Joseph. Soon, Joseph became chief of staff over all Potiphar's household. Then, Mrs. Potiphar began to change the atmosphere with her seductive ways and lustful intentions. Joseph was caught in a difficult place—he had to refuse the advances of his master's wife and yet fulfill the demands of his position. The day of confrontation required Joseph to make his decision. To maintain his integrity, he accepted his punishment and was sent to jail. Not exactly what he had in mind, but such was his life.

To his credit, Joseph was not swayed by these occurrences. He maintained his walk with the Lord and patiently waited for the fulfillment of his dreams. For a young man, far from home, cut off from his support systems, this was incredibly tough. Yet Joseph's sterling character shined through.

Like Joseph and his father, Jacob, you and I must determine to do things God's way. We must give up control of our lives and allow God to work His will in us. It's hard at times, but it is the only way God can get His work done in our lives. There are some reminders that should mark our anticipation of such an important decision to go God's way. Don't be misled—the Enemy is aware of our struggles. He will take advantage of every opportunity to keep us unsettled and insecure. As we forge ahead into God's way, keep these points in mind.

1. *Expect things to get worse before they get better.* From her appearance, I could tell the young woman before me had been weeping for some time. Her eyes and face spoke of the pain she bore. Her testimony reflected a bad marriage that was getting worse. She had an unresponsive husband who would not consider the Lord. Yet, there was an emerging hope when she spoke of her faith that God was going to work things out. She spoke with confidence of her anticipation that her husband would be a changed man when she got home.

As I listened to her, I felt prompted by the Spirit to say to her, "Be prepared. Things may get worse before they get better!" And they did. I know for some that would sound like defeatism, but understand that God works

His plans on His timetables—not ours! Instantaneous miracles are always possible and very much in order, but we must understand how God leads us through His process to complete healing and deliverance.

God told Abraham years before that his descendants would be strangers in a foreign land, but God would bring them back to the Promised Land. The completion of God's promise took more than 430 years (see Exodus 12:40). Ten generations passed before the promise was fulfilled. God was not slack, but He worked His will in His own timing.

Sometimes, our faith must carry us beyond what our circumstances indicate. We must learn not to panic or get alarmed when things go differently than we expect. God never forgets His promises. Too often, we allow our feelings to dictate our resolution. When we do, our feelings betray us. That's what Jacob was doing when he lamented, "All these things are against me" (42:36). From reading the account, we know that things were not against Jacob. In fact, things were working marvelously, but at that moment, he was feeling utter despair.

2. *Expect others to question and misunderstand you.* When we determine to walk by faith and not allow our circumstances to define who we are, we can anticipate that not everyone will understand. In some cases, you can anticipate them thinking you are crazy. It's interesting that God never reveals His truth in a crowded room with lots of witnesses. Have you ever noticed that? Those promises you hold dearly are often made in private. With no corroborating witness, you announce your assurance in God and your desire to walk faithfully with Him, and

the majority opinion is that you are off your rocker! The apostle Paul spoke to his bewildered shipmates in Acts 27 and revealed that an angel of God had let him know their future was secure. It was only Paul's testimony to the men. I am sure there were naysayers in the group, because the conditions and circumstances certainly did not back up Paul's confidence. When Joseph told his brothers and father about his dreams, they did not believe him. The dreams were so real to Joseph, he needed to share what God had revealed to him. There is nothing wrong with that. I have heard people say, "Joseph would have been better served to keep his dreams to himself."

I don't know. Evidently, Joseph felt it was important to testify of God's marvelous revelations. As a result, his brothers resented him and his father rebuked him. What did Joseph do? He held to his dreams. He never allowed his family to discourage his commitment to God's promise. His resilient attitude is an inspiration to any person who has ever had to stand alone in the face of criticism.

Job told his friends: "I have not sinned and this is not a punishment from God. I don't know why this happened, but I know God and He knows me. Our relationship is in good order and in the end, He will show Himself mighty!" Even his own wife nagged him, "Curse God and die!" (Job 2:9).

He refused to be swayed by those who did not understand. He knew God always kept His word. For Joseph, it was not a man who promised him a destiny—it was Jehovah God. Joseph's confidence in God enabled him to stand tall in the midst of others' attempts to dissuade him.

3. *Expect God to provide you with extraordinary strength to get through hard times.* Paul Lanier, my father-in-law, was a good man who died very young. My two sons did not have the opportunity to appreciate his attributes. A successful pastor and churchman, Paul had heart problems and died at the age of 59. He and his wonderful wife, Shirley, raised four children and were a tight-knit family. They were typical of people in their generation. She raised the children and he managed the family affairs and pastored the church. His passing placed an incredible burden on Shirley. She was not experienced with handling business for the family.

I was afraid that Shirley was not ready to live alone. Kathy and I encouraged her to move in with us. The other children did the same, but she refused. The place where she and Paul had lived was her home, and she determined to continue living there. From the beginning, the days were a great struggle, because her loss was great and the hours were long and lonely. Each member of the family tried to stay close, knowing she needed support. Her sons were there to help with the business affairs and the daughters gave strong moral support. The rest of us just prayed, hoped and waited, offering our love.

Now, the years have passed and Paul is still missed greatly. The emotions are still strong and certain memories still bring everyone to tears. The miracle is in the life of this woman who has risen above her doubts and difficulties.

She accepted her challenges admirably, not only to survive, but to flourish. Her adjustments have been many, but she is a great example of God's faithfulness.

Some time ago, while visiting, I hugged her and said, "Mom, you are a testimony to the grace of God!" God has kept her going. He enabled her to get up that first morning and begin her day. He gave her the courage to go on with her life. No child did that—it was God. A continued, sustaining strength from the hand of the Lord makes living tolerable and manageable. How do I know? I have experienced it. There have been times that seemed so unbearable with no visible way to survive— but we have survived. It was His sustaining grace that kept us going.

God is the reason you did not have a breakdown. The apostle Peter wrote to the beleaguered saints in Asia Minor, who were running for their very lives from Roman oppression, and spoke of the hope that beats in the heart of the believer:

> Who are protected by the power of God through faith for a salvation ready to be revealed in the last time. In this you greatly rejoice, even though now for a little while, if necessary, you have been distressed by various trials, that the proof of your faith, being more precious than gold which is perishable, even though tested by fire, may be found to result in praise and glory and honor at the revelation of Jesus Christ" (1 Peter 1:5-7).

You are still standing today because the power of God has sustained you. Count on it—God has committed to see you through. He wants you to be happy and He is pleased when you enjoy life. But His ultimate goal is to help you make it to the end. He knows the path ahead and what the requirements are. He may allow His children to go through rough waters at times to get to the next point, where He can complete His work in you.

4. *Expect to be personally amazed.* Have you ever been tempted to stand back and say "WOW!" when you considered the ways God has blessed and kept you? I have. Sometimes, I am totally overwhelmed when I realize how God takes care of me and never misses a detail.

The Lord's disciples were on a boat and about to be capsized. They were afraid, which is an indication of the storm's ferocity. In the midst of the storm, the disciples decided it was time to wake up Jesus. In doing so, they posed the question, "Teacher, do You not care that we are perishing?" (Mark 4:38). Jesus did not respond to the absurd question; rather He rebuked the wind and calmed the sea. The disciples' response was classic human nature: "Who then is this, that even the wind and the sea obey Him?" (v. 41).

You know how they felt. You have been there in the midst of a storm, when Jesus spoke words of peace to your soul and there was immediate relief. When that happens, there is no explanation and all we can say is "WOW!"

As you determine to do things God's way, you can anticipate that in moments of great need, He will amaze you. When it seems the end has come and there is nothing else to do, He shows up! On one occasion, the disciples had fished all night long and caught nothing. Jesus showed up and instructed them to cast their nets on the other side. Knowing the futility of such an action, they respectfully followed His advice, but were unprepared for the catch of fish in their nets. It was another amazing moment for Peter. When he saw the fish, he left them and came to the Lord. "But when Simon Peter saw that, he fell down at Jesus' feet, saying, 'Depart from me, for I am a sinful man, O Lord!' For amazement had seized him and all his companions because of the catch of fish which they had taken" (Luke 5:8, 9).

Where I was raised, we would say Peter was "blown away" by the miracle. I know the feeling. Often when we are at our lowest, Jesus comes in power and does great things, leaving us in total awe of His great power and might.

JUST TRANSFER

My youngest son, Jason, is an avid basketball player. Kathy and I have enjoyed watching him play in city recreation programs, middle school and high school. As a younger boy, he dreamed of playing basketball at the collegiate level. Unfortunately, he is cursed with the family height (shortness) and basketball is not the option he once hoped it would be.

During his middle school years, Jason struggled to make good grades in math. I remember especially in the eighth grade, his math homework was a struggle for everyone in our family. It did not resemble the eighth-grade math *I* had. Homework was a chore and many hours were spent by the entire family trying to help him through. He had the usual excuses: "The teacher doesn't like me"; "The work is too hard"; "There is not enough time for explanation in class." It was hard work, but in the end, he got a passing grade.

One night as he and I were completing his homework, he said, "Dad, something cool happened in school today. This kid in my math class was having trouble like I am and his mother got him transferred. You could do that for me!" I replied, "Oh really . . . so let me get this straight. You want me to have you transferred out of this math class into another math class?"

"No, not another math class—just out of math! I don't like math, Dad, and after all, this math stuff is not for me," he continued. Of course we never considered the transfer. But as I consider Joseph's life and the discomfort of his circumstances, I am reminded of Jason's remedy for eighth-grade math—*just transfer.*

We play the "transfer game." We go to God and tell Him we don't like our circumstances and we want out. We'll even quote the scripture that says we can have the desires of our heart. Let's put faith to the test and see what happens. Let's tell God to get us out and let us enjoy the freedom of other experiences. And what if God responded? We would be shouting and telling our friends how God delivered us from our struggles and allowed us to play all day. We never were comfortable, after all, in restrictions and confinement. Surely, God is not glorified in such nonsense. We would rejoice, and we would not be alone. There would always be someone ready to rejoice over our answered prayer.

However, there is a problem. Jason was going to the ninth grade next year. If he thought eighth-grade math was tough, he should have tried ninth-grade math without the eighth-grade experience. Do you see my point? While we may believe a miraculous deliverance from negative circumstances makes sense right now, we need to remember that we only see the present. God sees tomorrow. His knowledge of tomorrow guides His management of today. So don't be alarmed if God chooses not to deliver right now but gives the same advice He gave His servant Paul, "My grace is sufficient for you" (2 Corinthians 12:9). He knows how to get you through all your difficulties. He will mark your account with enough sustaining grace and strength for you to get on with life, whether your address is an Egyptian jail, a Canaanite tent, or Main Street, U.S.A.

Once Jacob turned loose of Benjamin and gave up his need to control and protect, he came to understand three things about God that we need to remember in our walk of faith:

- God is good.

- God is in control.

- God knows better than we do.

At first, I saw God as my observer, my judge, keeping track of the things I did wrong, so as to know whether I merited heaven or hell when I die. He was out there sort of like a president. But later on when I met Christ, it seemed as though life were rather like a bike ride, but it was a tandem bike and I noticed that Christ was in the back helping me pedal. I don't know just when it was that He suggested we change places, but life has not been the same since. When I had control, I knew the way. It was rather boring and predictable . . . it was the shortest distance between two points. But when He took the lead, He knew delightful long cuts, up mountain. Even though it looked like madness, He said "Pedal!" I worried and was anxious and asked, "Where are you taking me?" He laughed and did not answer, and I started to learn to trust. I forgot my boring life and entered into the adventure. And when I'd say "I'm scared," He'd lean back and touch my hand. He took me to people with gifts that I needed, gifts of healing, acceptance and joy. They gave me gifts to take on my journey, my Lord's and mine. And we were off again. He said "Give the gifts away; they're extra baggage, too much weight." So I did, to the people we met, and I found that in giving I received, and still our burden was light. I did not trust Him at first, in control of my life. I thought He'd wreck it but He knows bike secrets, knows how to make it bend to take sharp corners, knows how to jump to clear high rocks, knows how to fly to shorten scary passages. And I am learning to shut up and pedal in the strangest places and I'm beginning to enjoy the view and the cool breeze on my face with my delightful and constant companion, Jesus Christ. And when I'm sure I just can't do anymore, He just smiles and says "Pedal."[2]

Once Jacob placed his confidence in a God who had never failed him, he came to know blessings beyond his imagination. Because the next time he saw his sons, they were driving Egyptian wagons and telling their daddy, "You're not gonna believe this. Joseph is alive and Pharaoh says we can live there and enjoy the finest of the land."

You know, folks, sometimes you just have to shake your head and say, "WOW!"

*T*hen Joseph said to his brothers, "Please come closer to me." And they came closer. And he said, "I am your brother Joseph, whom you sold into Egypt. And now do not be grieved or angry with yourselves, because you sold me here; for God sent me before you to preserve life. For the famine has been in the land these two years, and there are still five years in which there will be neither plowing nor harvesting. And God sent me before you to preserve for you a remnant in the earth, and to keep you alive by a great deliverance."

Genesis 45:4-7

CHAPTER TEN

WHEN FORGIVENESS TAKES PLACE

D ebbie Cuevas was a 16-year-old girl in Madisonville, Louisiana, in 1980, when she and her boy-friend, Mark, were abducted at gunpoint by two men. Debbie was repeatedly raped and Mark was shot in the head and left for dead in a remote area of south Alabama. For a total of 30 hours, Debbie did not know if she would survive this ordeal, but miraculously she was released by her captors. Her testimony helped authorities prosecute the perpetrators. One of them, Robert Willie, was eventually executed in the Louisiana State Prison five years after his conviction. The other man was sentenced to life in prison without parole.

Even the justice of punishing these two vicious crimi-nals did not free Debbie from the prison of her own mind and emotions. She writes in her book, *Forgiving the*

145

Dead Man Walking, "For so many years, my reluctance to forgive was like a darkness inside, a barrier that barred joy and love and so many good things from my life. Forgiveness smashed that barrier and has enabled me to experience the giving and receiving of love again."[1]

Her story is a powerful example of how the hurts of our lives can trap us in a deep spiral of depression and despair. Debbie came to realize that forgiveness is hard work. Often we decide that it is easier *not* to forgive than to put forth the effort to be released from the awful prison of bitterness.

Have you ever made the statement, "I'll get even with you if it's the last thing I do!"? Many have. Think about that statement. Do you really want to spend the last moments of your life getting even with someone? I doubt it. I believe when faced with death, our thoughts are rarely focused on revenge.

When my father-in-law had his first open-heart surgery, I visited with him as soon as he was able to reflect on what had happened. I remember him telling me, "When they rolled me into the operating room, I instantly knew what was important to me. It wasn't the church I pastored, or the positions I held. What really mattered was my relationship with God and my family." Getting even is the last thing we would want to attempt when our lives are coming to an end. Yet, you probably know people who are consumed with revenge. Maybe it was a business partner who embezzled money or a spouse who chose another partner. Some fantasize about the day when they will . . .

- tell them off about what they did

- reciprocate

- make them pay for what happened.

Renee is a 911 operator in a small town in southeastern Alabama. One night she took a call that changed her life. In a fit of rage, a teenage boy had just shot his stepmother with a handgun. The woman was Renee's longtime best friend. The grief of losing her friend was almost too much to handle. She sent only one message to the boy—a short, handwritten note on the day of his mother's funeral, saying "I'm praying for you!" There was no response. Days turned into months, and then a year passed since her friend's death. Renee began to notice her feelings toward the boy had changed. She would admit to actually hating him. She wanted him to die. She hoped someone would do to him what he had done to his stepmother.

Renee's dilemma was further complicated because of her professed love for Christ. The guilt of her feelings was haunting. One night in a revival meeting, she heard a message on the forgiveness offered by Joseph toward his brothers. Renee decided to give her feelings of hate and resentment to the Lord. She cried bitter tears at the altar and received release from all the frustration and anguish she had carried for months. She related her story to me and announced, "God has taken my hatred away." That night I wept tears of joy as I realized what God had done for her. I tell you, only God can do that!

Joseph had every right to be angry about his treatment by his brothers, Potiphar's wife and his cellmates. Who could have blamed him if he had assembled the Egyptians, ridden across the desert, and wiped out the homes and families of his evil brothers?

Joseph wasn't concerned with any of that. I find the words of chapter 45 incredible. With tears of joy, Joseph revealed himself to his brothers, who did not recognize him. The years had not dampened his joy at seeing his brothers and restoring his relationship with them. Everything looked like it was set up for a major revenge. But Joseph refused to take advantage of the opportunity. Just as he refused Potiphar's wife, just as he refused to become bitter in prison, it was his choice. Over the years, Joseph developed an attitude to see all of life's moments in light of God's eternal plan. He even tells them, "Do not be afraid, for am I in God's place? And as for you, you meant evil against me, but God meant it for good in order to bring about this present result, to preserve many people alive" (Genesis 50:19, 20). This was his perspective. God was in control.

There is something sovereign at work in this young man's life. He understood that the power of God can transform the way we view things, people and circumstances. The years were long and the experiences brutal, but he did not become bitter and scarred. Remarkably, he rejoiced at God's ability to work His plan and reunite his family. Only God can change the way we form our opinions and deal with tribulation.

A young minister, who has been a personal friend of mine for years, made a terrible mistake and never told anyone about it. He tried to put it away and move on with his life. Eventually, someone did find out. In his heart, he truly believed the events of his past were forgiven by God and the parties involved. However, he became the object of someone else's revenge. History will probably reveal the accuser had no interest in justice, but was driven by personal jealousy of the young man's father. Unable to get even with the father, the accuser tried to ruin his son. He accomplished his goal, and the young man was punished. The young man accepted his guilt and punishment, yet the residual anger over the attitude of his accuser and the bitterness of how he was treated lingered. Days passed and finally a choice was made. He could spend his life agonizing over the wrong done to him or he could attempt to move on. He chose to move on.

Now, years later, it is so refreshing to hear him tell his story. As he recounts the disappointment over what happened, he adds, "There is no bitterness in my heart toward anyone. I cannot allow his actions to ruin my ministry. At some point, I had to decide to move on." To forgive those who have wronged us is the release that allows the floodgates of joy to open and the bitter waters of hatred and resentment to flow out.

Joseph had seen the light. God was never caught off-guard by anything that happened to him. He was always aware and had a plan. As His children, we can accept the promise: "No weapon that is formed against you shall prosper" (Isaiah 54:17). I can rest in the knowledge that

God is awesome and concerned about my well-being. He has set in place a plan for my deliverance. It was Joseph's understanding of God that allowed him to forgive his brothers.

Joseph did not wait for his brothers to ask his forgiveness. Some people wait their whole lives for the offender to come and beg forgiveness. In too many cases, it never happens.

So what do you do? You cannot allow others to hold the keys to your survival. Joseph had no idea he would ever see his brothers again; as far as he knew, he would not. So he could not wait for the day of revenge or recompense. He had to settle the issue internally—just him and his God.

I know people who are waiting for their offenders to crawl up and plead for forgiveness. They fantasize about the moment when the offender will be reduced to groveling and they will "get their day." As the old saying goes, don't hold your breath! You may be in for a long wait. Joseph did not wait. In his heart, his brothers were forgiven before they asked—even if they didn't! You and I cannot wait for someone else to trigger the release. If we want to find release from our frustration, forgiveness is the key. As you contemplate forgiving someone who has wronged you, keep these principles in mind.

1. *Forgiveness is costly.* When I extend forgiveness to those who offend me, whether they ask for it or not, I give up my right to get even. The only reason not to forgive is personal interest in "settling the score." When we choose to forgive, we give that up. It is one of the reasons so many of us struggle to forgive. We think we need to make our

case and see our offenders suffer. When Christ was hanging on the cross, He was exchanging His right to punish us for our sins for the right to forgive us and release us from penalty. In the same manner, our personal rights for revenge are released to a greater One, who promises to settle the score if it is needed.

> Never pay back evil for evil to anyone. Respect what is right in the sight of all men. If possible, so far as it depends on you, be at peace with all men. Never take your own revenge, beloved, but leave room for the wrath of God, for it is written, "Vengeance is Mine, I will repay," says the Lord (Romans 12:17-19).

2. *Refusing to forgive is hypocritical.* Jesus taught that forgiveness is both horizontal and vertical. You cannot have one without the other.

> "Our Father who art in heaven, hallowed be Thy name. Thy kingdom come. Thy will be done, on earth as it is in heaven. Give us this day our daily bread. And forgive us our debts, as we also have forgiven our debtors. And do not lead us into temptation, but deliver us from evil. (For Thine is the kingdom, and the power, and the glory, forever. Amen.)" For if you forgive men for their transgressions, your heavenly Father will also forgive you. But if you do not forgive men, then your Father will not forgive your transgressions (Matthew 6:9-15).

So we have a responsibility to forgive others—but it goes deeper. We cannot and should not expect to receive forgiveness from our heavenly Father if we are unwilling to forgive our fellow man. Jesus once told a story about a man who owed an enormous amount of money. He had no immediate means to repay it. Asking for mercy, his lender graciously granted him complete pardon and freed him from the crushing debt. What a moment to celebrate his release from this obligation!

Later, the one who had been forgiven went out and found a man who owed him an insignificant amount of money. The man likewise pleaded for time and consideration, but he was refused. Because the man could not pay, the forgiven man threw his debtor in jail. His friends were grieved at his indifference to the man. They told his lender what had happened.

> The summoning him, his lord said to him, "You wicked slave, I forgave you all that debt because you entreated me. Should you not also have had mercy on your fellow slave, even as I had mercy on you?" And his lord, moved with anger, handed him over to the torturers until he should repay all that was owed him (Matthew 18:32-34).

The latter state of this man was more distressful than the first. Now, in jail, he was completely helpless to correct his situation. How senseless to refuse others the treatment he had received. Again, Jesus left His disciples with the grave reminder: "So shall My heavenly Father also do to you, if each of you does not forgive his brother from your heart" (v. 35).

Forgiveness is not an option. We are commanded to forgive. It is not easy, but it is possible. Sometimes we cannot get over the hurt and frustration of our dilemma because we want someone to pay for doing wrong toward us. But Jesus paid for all sins—some of which will be committed against you!

3. *Forgiveness is God's business.* Each of us has experienced God's enablement to forgive, in spite of grave sin and wrongdoing. By nature, we are sinful humanity and deserve death. Jesus Christ came to earth in the form of human flesh, lived among us, died on a cross and allowed God the Father to embrace us, as if we had never done any wrong. That's why they call it "amazing grace." Only God can do that! But this story reveals something even more powerful. It shows that such forgiveness is possible between human beings when God is at work in us.

According to Scripture, when forgiveness is in order, the first step is always mine—regardless of what occurred. If I am the offender, my responsibility is obvious. "If therefore you are presenting your offering at the altar, and there remember that your brother has something against you, leave your offering there before the altar, and go your way; first be reconciled to your brother, and then come and present your offering" (Matthew 5:23, 24).

As I read Matthew 18:21-35, I recognize that when I am the offended, it is still my responsibility to forgive those who have wronged me, whether I am asked to or not. In either case, it is hard. Yet, if we are to be true servants of God, we must. To refuse to forgive would be hypocritical as Jesus' example in Matthew 18 reveals.

In every case in Scripture, we are taught that God forgives and shows mercy to sinners. We have been recipients of that grace, and our Father expects us to be equally forgiving to those who have offended us.

OVERCOMING BITTERNESS

There is something that usually hinders us in this area of forgiveness. It is our inherent belief that if we do right, we will always be rewarded. If we speed on the interstate, we don't like it when we see the blue light, but we know we deserve the ticket. However, if we are careful to observe the speed limit and still receive a ticket for something we know we did not do, we are not happy. We want vindication and we want someone to admit they were wrong. Contrary to our wishes, sometimes we are falsely accused and receive punishment for things we did not do. How do we get through the bitterness that inevitably follows? The following three additional principles about forgiveness have been forged out of my own experiences. I share them to encourage you to risk letting go and forgiving those who have caused you pain.

1. *Forgiveness is the release that begins the healing process.* I don't want to mislead you or create false hope in your heart. Those who have wronged you may never try to make things right, although that is what you desperately want. You cannot wait for them to make the first move. In your heart, you must allow the Holy Spirit to begin the process of healing by forgiving them before they attempt to make things right with you. It is hard and there is a tendency to want to savor the hurt and eventually get even. But believe me, the healing never starts until you accept God's grace in your heart and allow Him to help you forgive.

Dr. Robert Enright, Ph.D., professor of educational psychology at the University of Wisconsin at Madison, is the founder and president of the International Forgiveness Institute. Dr. Enright writes:

> When we are hurt emotionally, our first reactions are anger and a desire to get even with the person who inflicted the pain. We want the people who hurt us to suffer . . . while a willingness to forgive them is viewed as weakness. . . . But forgiveness is a powerful, courageous act that can ultimately be of great benefit to you and to those who are close to you. . . . Nursing a grudge takes an emotional toll. People who fail to forgive are more prone to depression, and the more resentment they harbor, the more depressed they are likely to become. . . . We resist forgiving because we misunderstand what forgiveness involves. Many of us think it means being a wimp letting the other person "off the hook" and inviting more mistreatment. . . . Letting go of a grudge is an exercise in personal power, not weakness. It puts you in control, not at the mercy of others. Forgiving others doesn't condone or excuse what he has done. By forgiving, you're not sheepishly accepting the action inflicted on you.[2]

2. *Unforgiveness breeds bitterness.* You have met them and so have I. Their faces tell the story. Listen to them for a moment and you can spot it. It is the acid of bitterness that settles in the heart, refusing to forgive. Right or wrong, only when the wrong suffered to the Lord's care is released can we be free from the awful poison of bitterness. "Pursue peace with all men, and the sanctification without which no one will see the Lord. See to it that no one comes short of the grace of God; that no root of bitterness springing up causes trouble, and by it many be defiled" (Hebrews 12:14, 15).

When I traveled to Israel, a guide took me to the Dead Sea. This massive body of water looks so tranquil and fresh, but it is bitter and poisonous. Because it has no outlet, nothing can leave. Fish cannot live in its waters and birds don't land there, because there is nothing but death in its stagnant depths. In the same way, the soul that harbors bitterness and never allows the Holy Spirit to blow freshness into it is also dead. Too many people have been poisoned by those who wronged them. In the final analysis, the most damaging wrong is done when they refuse to allow forgiveness to take out the hurts and bitterness of the soul. Believe me, friend, you cannot afford to do otherwise.

3. *The courage and power to forgive others who wrong us is a gift from God.* You and I cannot do this on our own. We don't just get up, forgive and move on. No, the hurts are too deep and personal. Lives have been rearranged and the future altered. Our ability to handle these situations is limited. We have to depend on Someone bigger than our hurts, who sees our lives in a different perspective. It is God who is able to make such miracles take place. In my own strength, I am suspect when it comes to letting God handle things. However, as I release my own right to fix situations, I find that He is able to heal my heart and handle the offenders.

In *Thoughts of a Christian Optimist*, William Arthur Wood offers this tremendous insight: "We are most like beasts when we kill. We are most like men when we judge. We are most like God when we forgive."[3]

When I totally release my wrongs and hurts to God, I get a different perspective of the matter altogether. The closer I get to God, the less interest I have in getting even. When I concentrate on loving God and letting Him be first in my life, I care less about what happens to the other person. God settles the issue when I allow Him to deal with them in whatever way He chooses! That is truly a miracle.

Nelson Mandela was a political prisoner in South Africa from 1963 until 1990. His release and the subsequent changeover from apartheid to democratic rule is one of the great stories of this century. In his book, *Great Souls: Six Who Changed the Century*, David Aikman, a former correspondent for *Time* magazine, writes:

> Many South Africans of all races played a role in ensuring the peaceful transfer of power. But without the extraordinary moral authority of the emerging South African black leader, Nelson Mandela, there would have been no central point or person around which such heroic efforts could coalesce. Mandela's moral authority was based on one simple virtue more than anything else: his willingness and capacity to forgive.[4]

Mandela, imprisoned by the South African government for more than 27 years because of his affiliation with the African National Congress, planned a violent overthrow of the "whites-only" segregationist government in his country. Their perception of this young black man was not wrong. His early days were filled with rage at the oppressive way his people were treated in South Africa. Remarkably, it was his imprisonment that saved his faith, his life and his countrymen. The long years in prison gave Mandela time to think and contemplate the days when he would be released. He was treated unkindly by some of the guards, while others were dramatically impacted by their encounters with Mandela. He refused to strike back, not allowing the acrimony of hurt to ruin his life. Released from prison in 1990, he and his countrymen changed the tide of public opinion about apartheid. His African National Congress began the negotiations for a transition of power to a democratically elected parliament and self-determination. It is reported that one of the major points in the negotiations was the perceived threat of the white government regarding retaliation by the blacks when they gained control of the state.

That is the way the world thinks. Like Joseph's brothers, the Africans who held the power understood all too well what hatred and resentment could do to those subjected to oppression. As history shows, their worries were unfounded. The man who spent more than two decades behind bars became a Christian and came to discover the power of prayer in his life.

Upon his release, Nelson Mandela sought to bring an entire nation together through forgiveness. As the newly-elected president of South Africa, he established the Truth and Reconciliation Commission, headed by Bishop Desmond Tutu, that offered amnesty to those who had committed crimes in the apartheid era. Within days, more than 3,000 applications for forgiveness were received and the deadline was extended. Mr. Aikman writes:

As we contemplate the story of Mandela, we see the virtue of forgiveness emerging again and again. Forgiveness always requires a conscious choice rather than a feeling and there must have been times when Mandela consciously chose to forgive people for whom he had anything but natural empathy. There had to be incidents of injustice, brutality and deprival to which forgiveness seemed a weak and unsatisfying response. It cannot always have come easily to him. Yet, decade after decade, Mandela chose to forgive. . . . Mandela could have, after all, made his willingness to sit down with the enforcers of apartheid subject to a great wall of conditions. Those enforcers had oppressed his own people for centuries. But forgiveness is supremely a Christian virtue. Unless it is conferred on others without demanding anything in return, it is not genuine. . . . Mandela forgave unconditionally. And he chose to believe that by displaying dignity and by consciously withholding animosity, he could accomplish far more than he could possibly achieve armed with a fistful of ultimatums and threats. Although his beliefs ran against the grain of post-Christian logic of the twentieth century, Mandela was right.[5]

When God works in the lives of men and women, they can literally change the course of history. He can change the atmosphere in a bad marriage or a soured relationship. He can bring freshness to broken families and destroyed friendships. God, at work in our lives, drains the bitter resentment that resolves to get even. We must be determined to move on.

Joseph's perspective was not to get even, although every member of his family was worried he would. I am amused when I read the words, "Then Joseph said to his brothers, 'I am Joseph! Is my father still alive?' But his brothers could not answer him, for they were dismayed at his presence" (Genesis 45:3).

Can you imagine what they thought when they recognized him? It had been more than 22 years, but they still remembered what had happened the last time they were together. They must have been consumed with guilt over what they had done. Their mental questions must have been, *What will he do to us now? How could this be?* While they were worried about payback coming, Joseph knew God had bigger plans. He had already forgiven them.

In the same way, we were forgiven by our heavenly Father, who paid for our sins before we ever committed them. Such forgiveness is shown to us in the account recorded in John 13. This was the last time the disciples would be together. The end was near and Jesus knew it. They had gathered for the Last Supper. The disciples did not yet realize the gravity of the moment. The Lord girded Himself with a towel and began to wash the feet of His disciples—an act reserved for the very lowest of servants. Yet, the Master of the Universe washed the feet of these men. But the heart of Christ was most notably revealed in His treatment of Judas. Max Lucado renders it this way:

> I looked for a Bible translation that read, "Jesus washed all the disciples' feet except the feet of Judas," but I couldn't find one. What a passionate moment when Jesus silently lifts the feet of his betrayer and washes them in the basin! Within hours, the feet of Judas, cleansed by the kindness of the one he will betray, will stand in Caiaphas's court. Behold the gift Jesus gives his followers! He knows what these men are about to do. He

knows they are about to perform the vilest act of their lives. By morning they will bury their heads in shame and look down at their feet in disgust. And when they do, he wants them to remember how his knees knelt down before them and he washed their feet. He wants them to realize those feet are still clean. "What I am doing you do not understand now, but you will know after this." He forgave their sin before they even committed it. He offered mercy before they even sought it.[6]

Except for the promises of God, Joseph had no idea this moment would come. In his heart the issue was over long before his brothers came to his house. Even Jacob, his father, was concerned that Joseph would turn on his brothers. Years later, Jacob died and all of his family returned to Canaan to bury him. When they returned to Egypt, the brothers sent messengers to Joseph to share their father's request concerning the brothers' evil. That is the way the world operates: "Do unto others as they have done unto you!" Their action moved Joseph to tears. His words are some of the most memorable of his life story. Read them slowly and contemplate the applicable spiritual truth they hold:

> When Joseph's brothers saw that their father was dead, they said, "Perhaps Joseph will hate us, and may actually repay us for all the evil which we did to him!" So they sent messengers to Joseph, saying, "Before your father died he commanded, saying, 'Thus you shall say to Joseph, "I beg you, please forgive the trespass of your brothers and their sin; for they did evil to you."' Now, please, forgive the trespass of the servants of the God of your father." And Joseph wept when they spoke to him. Then his brothers also went and fell down before his face, and they said, "Behold, we are your servants." Joseph said to them, "Do not be afraid, for am I in the

place of God? But as for you, you meant evil against me; but God meant it for good, in order to bring it about as it is this day, to save many people alive. Now therefore, do not be afraid; I will provide for you and your little ones." And he comforted them and spoke kindly to them (Genesis 50:15-21, *NKJV*).

I can hardly read those verses without feeling emotion. Jacob's sons operated from a system of values that required a penalty. When their sister Dinah was raped by the Hivites, they conspired to exact revenge. That's what they expected from Joseph. It had been years, and they were still waiting for him to drop the hammer on them. Why? Because of their guilt.

So many people today cannot accept the reality that God paid for their sins when He gave His Son. Their concept of God is skewed by their relationships with others. They think wrongs deserve punishment, but it doesn't have to be that way with God. With our multitude of transgressions casting a shadow on eternity, God offered Jesus as a payment and forgave us completely. Not only did He provide for my redemption, but He did so before I ever asked. Remember the apostle Paul's words, "But God demonstrates His own love toward us, in that while we were yet sinners, Christ died for us" (Romans 5:8).

As we close this remarkable chapter of Joseph's life, we need to remind ourselves of God's ultimate sovereignty. Nothing escapes His watchful eyes. Although you may feel terribly alone in your hurts and frustrations, you are not. Sometimes when I hurt, I don't see things as clearly as they are. The young lady I introduced at the beginning of this chapter felt great despair toward God and wondered, *How could God allow me to be raped three times by those vicious men? If God is real, why didn't He stop them?* These are legitimate questions. However, keep in mind that God never leaves us alone without His grace and strength to manage even the darkest moments of our lives. Debbie writes, "The more I thought about it, the more I looked back through my new faith-tinted lenses, the more I began to see. Not only had God been with me at my lowest, most desperate moments, he had also uniquely equipped me to survive everything I'd been through before and since my horrible kidnaping ordeal."[7]

If you feel the harsh blow of a horrible deed done to hurt and abuse you, you are not alone. The sustaining grace of God heals and enables you to survive. Forgiveness is a remarkable gift from God to the hurting.

163

"Hurry and go up to my father, and say to him, 'Thus says your son Joseph, "God has made me lord of all Egypt; come down to me, do not delay. And you shall live in the land of Goshen, and you shall be near me, you and your children and your children's children and your flocks and your herds and all that you have. There I will also provide for you, for there are still five years of famine to come, lest you and your household and all that you have be impoverished."' And behold, your eyes see, and the eyes of my brother Benjamin see, that it is my mouth which is speaking to you. Now you must tell my father of all my splendor in Egypt, and all that you have seen; and you must hurry and bring my father down here. . . ." Then Pharaoh said to Joseph, "Say to your brothers, 'Do this: load your beasts and go to the land of Canaan, and take your father and your households and come to me, and I will give you the best of the land of Egypt and you shall eat the fat of the land. Now you are ordered, 'Do this: take wagons from the land of Egypt for your little ones and your wives, and bring your father and come. And do not concern yourselves with your goods, for the best of all the land of Egypt is yours.' "

Genesis 45:9-13, 17-20

Chapter Eleven

When You Are Blessed in Spite of Yourself

My oldest son, Jeremy, and I are avid readers. Fortunately, we like many of the same books. Our favorites are the John Grisham novels. Over the years, one of us (usually Dad) will buy the latest and we will read it simultaneously. Each of us has our own bookmark and we read at our own pace and talk about where we are in the book, discussing the upcoming chapters if one of us is ahead. We have had a blast over the years reading and talking about these books. We have our own personal favorites. We eagerly await each new novel. As long as Grisham keeps writing them, I can assure you Jeremy and I will keep reading them.

One of the latest has an unexpected ending that drove us crazy. I reached the end first and, not wanting to spoil it for him, I said nothing. One night as I passed his room, I noticed him reading the novel. Moments later, I heard him squeal and come running into my room. "What a great ending to that book!" he said.

While I did not care for the ending (mainly because I had not considered it a possibility), I was intrigued by his pleasure. "Well, I didn't think it would end that way," he said.

Interesting how things turn out. As we conclude the story of Joseph, we come to an unimaginable ending to Joseph's long journey and it brings joy to our hearts. Remember, many years had passed. His life has had many ups and downs, just like yours and mine. But Joseph faithfully kept his eyes on the Lord during all these years. Now, as the Biblical record is about to end, we find Joseph living in the blessings of the Lord. His life came full circle and God brought about the most glorious ending.

Four things become evident as we reach the end of Joseph's story:

- Joseph saw the fulfillment of his dreams.
- Jacob was reunited with his son.
- His brothers found peace in their relationship with Joseph.
- The famine did not destroy the family of Jacob.

As readers of the story, we had the opportunity of knowing somewhat how it was going to end. We know Joseph had a glorious reunion with his family, his father and all that he missed those many years.

Joseph did not have this insight. He did not know how it was going to turn out. His only hope was his never-ending faith in God and His promises. Joseph's journey was difficult. He got up each morning and faced whatever was out there, trusting God for the grace to manage. He knew that there was never a moment when God was not watching out for him. It is the same for us today.

In his book, *Created to Be God's Friend*, Henry T. Blackaby discusses God's relationship with Abraham. He follows this line of thinking and cautions us to remember to view the Bible and its characters through the eyes of God.

> One cannot understand the unfolding of God's eternal purpose in time, without seeing the Bible from God's perspective! The Bible is the record of God. It reveals the unfolding of His eternal purposes in time, especially through those He chooses and calls to Himself. His purpose in recording it in Scripture is that all those who read of the wonderful works of God would instinctively ready themselves to be encountered by God. Therefore, Genesis does not reveal Abram's walk with God (though you can read and study it for profit that way), but rather Genesis opens to our understanding the activity of God in and through a man called Abram. We cannot understand Abram's walk with God unless we see it as God sees it![1]

Clarence Jump came into my life in a most bizarre way. One evening, as my family and I were leaving for a revival at a neighboring church, I received a phone call from a retired minister who lived in our community. He asked if I would have prayer with his son. Clarence had been traumatized by an attempted robbery just hours earlier. Two men had come to the gas station where he worked and demanded money. They forced Clarence to lie on the floor, prepared to kill him if he did not obey their demands. They had placed a loaded pistol against Clarence's skull. Later, he confessed to me that in that moment, he knew if they pulled the trigger, he would spend eternity in hell. This backslidden preacher's son had run out of options. A quick, whispered prayer to God was all Clarence had going for him—or so he thought.

Remarkably, the robbers got their money and left Clarence lying on the floor, trembling. After completing the police report and working with a sketch artist, Clarence came home and sought a preacher to pray with him. He intended to keep the promise he had made to God. He would turn his life around. That's where I came in.

As he walked into my house, Clarence Jump looked every bit like a man who had stared eternity in the face and had blinked. Fear was in his eyes. After some time, we prayed and, in our living room, Clarence Jump came to know Christ as his personal Savior. For the next two years, he and his wife, Ann, were faithful and loyal members of our church. They grew attached to my oldest son and we spent many enjoyable hours with the Jump family.

One Sunday after church, Clarence indicated that he would be checking into the hospital for a test and possible surgery. "It's nothing serious," he assured me. "There's no need to worry."

On the day of the surgery, I met with the family for prayer. Everyone seemed to have peace. The reports indicated that Clarence had an intestinal blockage.

Waiting with families in such situations is what pastors do routinely. You come to understand how surgery processes work and that each hospital has its own procedure for updates. A short time after the family had settled in the waiting area, a Red Cross volunteer came and announced a phone call for me. When I got to the telephone the surgeon spoke very softly, "Bring Mr. Jump's wife to the operating room on the second floor and no one else . . . don't delay!"

He hung up before I could respond. I was stunned. Had he died on the table? What could have gone wrong? In such cases, doctors don't play games—they act. So I followed his instructions. Together Ann and I moved up to the second floor. The doctor met us and the word he gave us was cancer. It was extensive and inoperable— there was no chance of survival. He estimated that Clarence had less than two months to live. There is not much that prepares anyone for such an impact. You feel like you have been hit by a truck. This Christian doctor asked me to join him in prayer. Together we would tell Clarence in the morning when he awoke from the surgery.

It was my first church, and only my second experience helping people deal with death. As the son of a minister, I thought I was prepared for everything, but I was totally unprepared for my role the next morning. Clarence was my friend, my member and a brother in

Christ. I knew he would look for his pastor to bring a "word from the Lord." All night, I tossed and turned, sleeping very little. I awakened well before dawn and dressed for the appointment. I felt dread in my heart.

How was I to tell a man who has just started to live that, unless something miraculous occurred, he was going to die? I prayed and asked the Lord for something to strengthen my friend. I received nothing. I had talked with my father, who has been a pastor most of my life. Though he tried to encourage me to trust in the Lord—nothing came.

The drive to the hospital took 10 minutes. Sitting at the red light just three blocks from the hospital, God spoke to me. As I waited for the light, I remembered how the children of Israel wanted bread to eat and had none. God prepared a substance called manna for them. Each morning they would gather it and prepare it for their bread. The instructions were clear—gather only what you need for today, because this bread would not last for two days. If they tried to store it, it would rot. Only on the Sabbath could they gather a two-day supply of manna. The lesson for them was the message God prepared in my heart that morning for my dying friend: "Don't attempt to live any further than this moment. Trust God for every day." Cancer or not, it is the only way God operates. He promises us His abiding and sustaining grace for each day—but only for that day.

That's God's choice. We have His promise if we are privileged to rise another day—He will again supply His grace to get us through whatever we have to face.

For Clarence, it was the treatments and the medication, the pain and the slow, torturous agony of cancer. For you, it may be your stressful job, your marriage relationship, the small children you are raising alone, or any number of things. You cannot do it alone. You must have God's grace that comes from trusting Him.

That's what Joseph did. He got up each morning and trusted God with the details, living each day with the anticipation that God was sufficient for His needs. What a way to live!

The ending of this story brings tears to my eyes when I realize how much Joseph endured, how much he trusted, how long he waited, and how much God blessed him. He had been a slave boy on an auction block with no appreciable value, but now he said to the brothers who had sent him there, "Tell my father of all my splendor in Egypt, and all that you have seen" (Genesis 45:13).

Who would have believed that a pauper could become a powerful ruler with wealth and authority. . . and he was willing to share his wealth with his family— the very ones who had treated him so horribly.

As I consider God's blessings on Joseph, I realize he is not the only one in this saga who was blessed by God. Blessings rest on almost every character we read about. They seem to fall into the following categories.

THE UNLIKELY
Potiphar, the jailer and Pharaoh make up this group. Each of them was the recipient of blessings in some degree because of their association with Joseph.

The account gives us this information regarding Joseph's relationship with Potiphar:

> And his master saw that the Lord was with him and that the Lord made all he did to prosper in his hand. So Joseph found favor in his sight, and served him. Then he made him overseer of his house, and all that he had he put under his authority. So it was, from the time that he had made him overseer of his house and all that he had, that the Lord blessed the Egyptian's house for Joseph's sake; and the blessing of the Lord was on all that he had in the house and in the field. Thus he left all that he had in Joseph's hand, and he did not know what he had except for the bread which he ate (Genesis 39:3-6, *NKJV*).

Potiphar was not the only one blessed by the life of Joseph. The jailer, although not mentioned by name, was also influenced by this man. During Joseph's imprisonment, things in the jail went smoothly and the jailer's workload decreased because Joseph was blessed of God.

Pharaoh was also blessed because of Joseph's life and influence. When his wise men failed to interpret his dreams, God led him to look to Joseph. From the moment he met Joseph, he found a man who was trustworthy and capable. Joseph brilliantly organized the harvest and planned for the coming famine. Pharaoh and his kingdom were spared devastation because of the blessings of God through Joseph.

All of these individuals did not deserve God's blessings, yet they enjoyed them. Each of them was able to benefit from God's presence in the life of Joseph. You call these the "unlikely" blessed of God! But don't we all fit in this category to some degree? In spite of our past, God still pours out His grace and favor upon those who choose to accept Him. I believe God likes to unpredictably bless the unlikely.

THE UNDESERVING

This group consists of the brothers of Joseph. These men were thoroughly undeserving of God's blessings. In my opinion, they should not have benefited from God's graces in this matter. But I'm not God!

These men despised Joseph, selling their own brother into slavery. Then they conspired to lie to their father about Joseph's fate, plunging their father into grief for 22 years, never backing down from their initial lie. How many nights did Jacob cry and mourn the loss of his son? Yet, his grief was unnecessary!

In spite of their deceit and selfishness, God still poured out incredible blessings on them and their families at the end of this story.

> Then Pharaoh said to Joseph, "Say to your brothers, 'Do this: load your beasts and go to the land of Canaan, and take your father and your households and come to me, and I will give you the best of the land of Egypt and you shall eat the fat of the land. Now you are ordered, 'Do this: take wagons from the land of Egypt for your little ones and your wives, and bring your father and come. Also do not concern yourselves with your goods, for the best of all the land of Egypt is yours.' " (Genesis 45:17-20).

They were invited by Pharaoh to come to Egypt with their families and live in splendor. I find it interesting that Pharaoh told Joseph to instruct them not to even pack a thing—just come! All of the good of the land was theirs. What blessings to those who seemed so undeserving!

It is here where you and I sometimes have problems. We don't mind reading about good people who do nice things being blessed. But when a wicked person is blessed, we get upset. When I read about Ted Bundy's salvation testimony, I paused and wondered. He was such an evil man who had murdered many innocent people. Yet, according to his testimony, Ted Bundy found peace with God before he died. Recently, I listened to a radio report about David Berkowitz, the purported "Son of Sam" killer, who killed several people in New York City some years ago. According to Dr. D. James Kennedy's interview with him, he was marvelously saved.

How do you explain this? I can't—I don't even try to. All I know is that God is God and He never gives up on us. He is unconcerned with public opinions and my personal bias about whom He should and should not bless. He blesses even those who don't deserve His blessings.

He did the same for you and me. He did not take into account our sinful past, but He accepted us as sons and daughters by His grace and allows us to enjoy the privileges of His goodness. We certainly do not deserve His blessings. Paul explains it like this:

> For while we were still helpless, at the right time Christ died for the ungodly. For one will hardly die for a righteous man; though perhaps for the good man someone would dare even to die. But God demonstrates His own

love toward us, in that while we were yet sinners, Christ died for us (Romans 5:6-8).

There is an incredible example of this kind of grace in 2 Samuel 9. Before David became king, he made a vow to his young friend, Jonathan, that when he became king, he would show kindness to his household. When he became king upon Saul's death, the family of Saul fled for their lives, fearing David would kill them. The son of Jonathan, Mephibosheth, was the unfortunate victim of a fall in his early childhood. The fall left him lame for the rest of his life. He lived in seclusion in a desert place called Lo Debar. He went from being a king's kid one moment to a nobody living in "nowhere-ville."

Then one day, David remembered his promise and inquired about the family of Saul. After hearing about Mephibosheth, David summoned him. Fearing that his life was in jeopardy, the crippled man came humbly and fell before the king. Quite to his amazement, the king's orders were not judgment—they were a blessing. All his father's former wealth and possessions were restored to him by the king's edict. He was brought to the king's palace to sit at the table with King David. He became a recipient of the good graces of the one who could have killed him.

I sometimes meet people who act like they did God a favor when they accepted salvation! They boast of their former lives as if they held great promise. In reality, we were all destined for eternal punishment. There was nothing we could do to find redemption.

Like Mephibosheth, we were destitute and living far from the King's table. The dead-end feelings of our life revealed the true nature of our sinful past. Then, the Holy Spirit invited us to be restored to our rightful position as sons and daughters of the King. He forgave our sins, placed His righteousness in our hearts and invited us to sit at His table, even though we did not deserve it! Now when He views us, He doesn't see our righteousness, but that of His Son, Jesus Christ.

The Unexpecting

Jacob was a man whose family was fractured. For more than 20 years, he had mourned Joseph's "death." His wife had died prematurely, one son was gone, and now Simeon was being held captive in Egypt. What Jacob did not know was that his sorrow was about to be turned to joy. His hopelessness and despair had almost overwhelmed him. Life had been cruel and the result was bitterness and frustration. Questions filled his mind and he had few answers.

Imagine what must have occurred in his heart when he heard the hoofbeats of the horses and the wheels of Pharaoh's carts coming up the road. His sons began to excitedly exclaim, "Joseph is alive! He has sent for us!" It was almost more than the old man could take. However, after all these years of disappointment, he looked at the carts of Pharaoh and knew they were not his own. He saw the excitement in the faces of his sons and heard the sincerity of their report. Could it be true? Was Joseph alive?

He should have remembered the promise of God many years before at Bethel:

> He dreamed, and behold, a ladder was set up on the earth, and its top reached to heaven; and there the angels of God were ascending and descending on it. And behold, the Lord stood above it and said: "I am the Lord God of Abraham your father and the God of Isaac; the land on which you lie I will give to you and your descendants. Also your descendants shall be as the dust of the earth; you shall spread abroad to the west and the east, to the north and the south; and in you and in your seed all the families of the earth shall be blessed. Behold, I am with you and will keep you wherever you go, and will bring you back to this land; for I will not leave you until I have done what I have spoken to you" (Genesis 28:12-15, *NKJV*).

I would like to tell him, "Jacob, God keeps His word. You were never out of His sight. He has been working His plan to preserve you all these years. When you thought things were as bad as they could get, God was writing an incredible ending for your life!"

THE UNSHAKEN

Joseph, the young man who never gave up hope in his God, ends up in this category. He did not let his circumstances define him, but he kept his dreams in focus. As a result, when he came to the end of his life, the blessings of God were literally overtaking him—coming faster than he could process them.

A good friend of mine once called me at a crucial time in my life. I was discouraged about my church and my ministry. Things were not going well and problems were developing in the church. The evening he called, he did not know just how much I needed that pep talk. Over a meal, he asked me a very probing question. Although it has been more than 15 years, I have never forgotten it: "When Joseph was sold by his brothers to the Ishmaelite traders and taken to Egypt, what would Joseph have said was the worst day of his life?"

"Well, I guess he would say the day his brothers sold him into slavery."

"You are probably right," he said. "But, after it was all over and he was reunited with his family and enjoying the blessings of God, if you asked him what was the most important day of his life, he might have said the day his brothers sold him into slavery!"

What we sometimes think are the darkest moments of our lives are merely the catalysts propelling us toward unbelievable blessings. With human eyes and minds, we cannot comprehend what God does, so we often jump to incorrect conclusions. Our great big God is always in control. What the Enemy may attempt to do and what God allows him to do may appear to be tragic, but God knows best. His eye is on your tomorrow and His knowledge of tomorrow guides our lives. Right at this moment, He can see the glorious ending. Wait for Him. Joseph did and he lived to enjoy the blessings of God in spite of everything and everybody who got in his way. For the rest of his life, he enjoyed God's blessings and rejoiced in what God had done. Joseph was once again in the bosom of his family. His fantastic dreams had been realized. He ended up a long way from home, but he made it—with God.

> Now Joseph stayed in Egypt, he and his father's household, and Joseph lived one hundred and ten years. And Joseph saw the third generation of Ephraim's sons; also the sons of Machir, the son of Manasseh, were born on Joseph's knees. . . . So Joseph died at the age of one hundred and ten years; and he was embalmed and placed in a coffin in Egypt (Genesis 50:22, 23, 26).

The final chapters must be played out. God is not contained to time or space as we are. He exists in your life, both now and tomorrow, orchestrating it all. Every detail is coming together; when the final piece falls into place, it will be a grand masterpiece, far beyond what you might have imagined.

Yes, there is a better day coming. As we leave the story of Joseph, I am reminded of two powerful passages that speak to you and me today. One is from an Old Testament prophet who reminded Israel of the greatness that remained to be revealed. The other is the Revelator's review of what he saw in the last chapter of the Revelation. As you read, imagine the glorious end. Keep hoping, dreaming and believing.

> "Behold, days are coming," declares the Lord, "When the plowman will overtake the reaper and the treader of grapes him who sows seed; when the mountains will drip sweet wine, and all the hills will be dissolved. Also I will restore the captivity of My people Israel, and they will rebuild the ruined cities and live in them, they will also plant vineyards and drink their wine, and make gardens and eat their fruit. I will also plant them on their

land, and they will not again be rooted out from their land which I have given them," says the Lord your God (Amos 9:13-15).

And He showed me a river of the water of life, clear as crystal, coming from the throne of God and of the Lamb, in the middle of its street. And on either side of the river was the tree of life, bearing twelve kinds of fruit, yielding its fruit every month; and the leaves of the tree were for the healing of the nations. And there shall no longer be any curse; and the throne of God and of the Lamb shall be in it, and His bond-servants shall serve Him; and they shall see His face, and His name shall be on their foreheads. And there shall no longer be any night; and they shall not have need of the light of a lamp nor light of the sun, because the Lord God shall illumine them; and they shall reign forever and ever (Revelation 22:1-5).

The years came and went, and soon, there were few people who remembered Joseph or were alive to tell of what happened in his life. Among the many who died daily in Egypt, he was viewed by the general population as nothing more than a passing generation of leadership. But God did not forget. He wrote it all in a book that would be read for thousands of years because He wanted people like you and me to be reminded of God's consistent attention to the needs and situations of His children. He never loses sight of any of them, not for a moment. Your situations are right before Him. If you trust Him, the ending will be better than any novel ever written.

ENDNOTES

Chapter 2

[1]*Discipleship Journal*, Jan. 1999:109.

[2]Andy Stanley, *Visioneering* (Sisters, OR: Multnomah, 1999) 151.

Chapter 3

[1]Ron Mehl, *God Works the Night Shift* (Sisters, OR: Multnomah, 1995) 18.

[2]David Hazard, *"His Ways, Our Ways,"* *Discipleship Journal*, Issue 95, 1996: 46.

[3]Oswald Chambers, *My Utmost for His Highest* (Grand Rapids: Discovery House, 1992).

[4]*Inspire@inspiree.infoadvn.com*; 10/25/99.

[5]Jim Cymbala, *Fresh Wind, Fresh Fire* (Grand Rapids: Zondervan, 1997) 119.

[6]*Discipleship Journal*, Issue 155, 1998.

Chapter 4

[1]Randy Alcorn, "Consequences of a Moral Tumble," *Leadership*, Summer 1988: 46.

Chapter 5

[1]David Aikman, *Great Souls: Six Who Changed the Century* (Nashville: Word, 1998).

[2]Malcolm Muggeridge, *A Twentieth Century Testimony* (Nashville: Thomas Nelson, 1978).

[3]Oswald Chambers, *My Utmost for His Highest* (Grand Rapids: Discovery House, 1935, renewed 1963).

Chapter 7
[1]Charles Swindoll, *The Mystery of God's Will* (Nashville: Word, 1999) 17.

Chapter 9
[1]*Discipleship Journal*, Issue 95, 1996: 52.

[2]Tim Hansel, *Holy Sweat: The Remarkable Things Ordinary People Can Do When They Let God Use Them!* (Nashville: Word, 1987).

Chapter 10
[1]Debbie Morris with Gregg Lewis, *Forgiving the Dead Man Walking* (Grand Rapids: Zondervan, 1998) 250.

[2]Dr. Robert Enright, "Forgiveness and Your Health," *Bottom Line Personal*, Nov. 15, 1999.

[3]Charles R. Swindoll, *The Tale of the Tardy Oxcart and 1,501 Other Stories* (Nashville: Word, 1998) 216.

[4]David Aikman, *Great Souls: Six Who Changed the Century* (Nashville: Word, 1998) 66.

[5]Aikman, 12.

[6]Max Lucado, *Just Like Jesus* (Nashville: Word, 1999) 16.

[7]Morris, 222.

Chapter 11
[1]Henry T. Blackaby, *Created to Be God's Friend* (Nashville: Thomas Nelson, 2000) 6.